Sketches

The Wednesday Poems

Published by 99% Press,

an imprint of Lasavia Publishing Ltd.

Auckland, New Zealand

www.lasaviapublishing.com

ISBN: 978-1-99-118985-1

Sketches

The Wednesday Poems

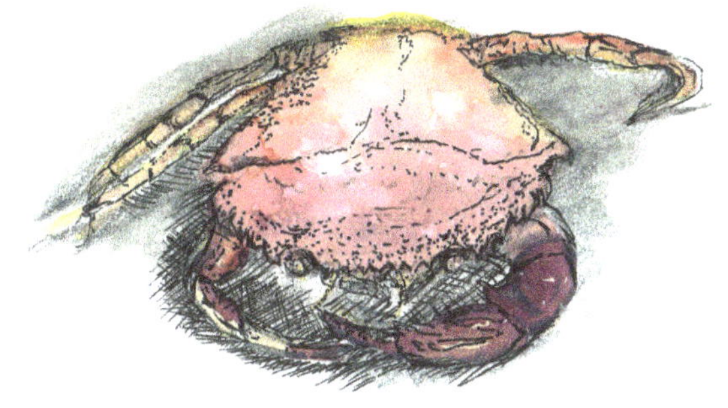

Mike Johnson

Leila Lees

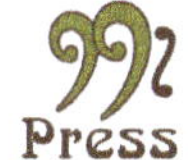

Forword

We live in the age of islands, and Mike Johnson's chosen island is Waiheke in the Hauraki Gulf, which he spans with his poems. Quizzing the landscape with pen and notebook, anything is possible. Out of a cross hatching of words, magic might happen. Sketches, a gathering of immediate impressions in poetry and artworks, is about ways of seeing — that is, transcendent seeing, registering the insistent is-ness of the world. Mike Johnson's atmospheric sketches are the poetic language of an acute observer, evoking the hidden interior life of things in quick, informal, but revealing and imagistic snapshots. In Sketches,

> 'the delicate paspalum
> talks to itself
> as it grows heavy'

and

> 'a white mushroom glows
> with its own strength'

Above all, the poet declares,

> 'we are but a song
> stretched over bone'

Sketches, a skein of fleeting moments arrested on the page, manages with its glancing, darting reflections and philosophical perceptions, to find just the right formulation to deliver a descriptive vitalism that is open, alert, tentative, ambulatory, elegant, palpable.

David Eggleton, Poet Laureate, 2019 – 2022

Sketches Preface:
The Wednesday Poems

The poems in Sketches were put onto Facebook each week as a Wednesday Poem. The first poem went up on June 15 2019, and the last one went up on June 30, 2021. Each poem was accompanied by an artwork from Leila Lees. I was impressed how, when we went for our walks through some of our favourite places, Leila could so quickly sketch what she saw, and I began to do the same with words. It was a new experience, to write lines outside, on location, sometimes standing up on a beach or headland, writing quickly without too much thought. I left these raw lines as they were, without turning them into well-made poems. My intention was to capture the fleeting impressions of the moment. They remain word sketches. Perhaps I could have used these lines to create 'real poems' but I'm always mindful of master sketcher Robert Creeley who once asked, 'Is that a real poem or did you just make it up?'

Mike Johnson, Waiheke Island, March 2023

Contents

COASTLINES   11

Wainui   Matariki 2019   13

Matarangi   17

Whakanewha, Waiheke Island   27

Onetangi, Waiheke Island   49

Dead Dog Bay, Waiheke Island   59

Matapana (Palm Beach), Waiheke Island   69

Oneroa, Waiheke Island   81

Piha   87

INTERIORS   91

The Past   98

Tongariro   115

Crescent Valley   125

Let There Be   139

Love and Chains   155

Coastlines

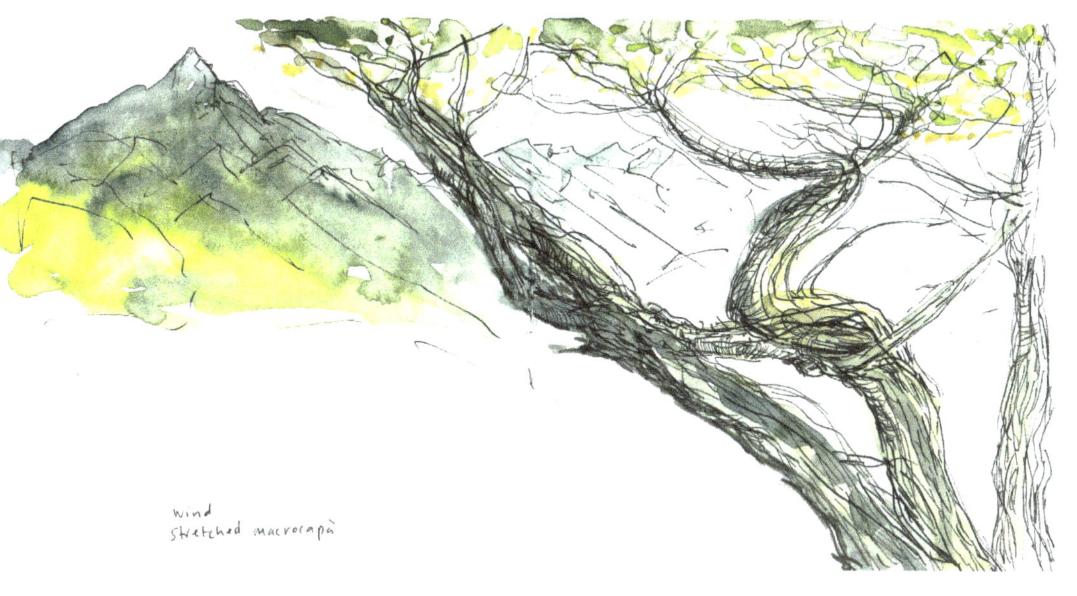

WAINUI

Matariki 2019

off track

as you love to do
you lead us off track
over a muddy pasture
along a fence line
electrified
and barbed
past a barn with no name
mysterious and stark

up, over
and around
you find a path
that isn't a path
until you find it

always the trail-blazer
me grumbling along behind
adventure in the wind
a river to cross that comes up
over the knees
a hill to climb that has no summit
a horizon that has no line
a beach that has no tides
but the ones we follow

'how do we get home,' I ask
'We'll just take the road,' you say

cliff edge

we find a seat sheltered from the morning gale
after the drama of the hat
that raced for the cliff
with a head full of wind
we sit there
as if it were meant to be
and consider the view
cabbage trees, spiky as a bottle brush
flax slapping the wind about
receding headlands
a pool of spreading light
from a dark horizon
Karioi, half submerged
in raincloud, like a submarine
you draw, I write
the world ducks and weaves
we find other things to talk about
black-backed gulls
twist and slide, their precarious
play

labyrinth

looking for you
I find a path I've never walked
through tall trees, manicured lawns
and empty pagodas

like the well-kept grounds
of a private estate

around the path goes
crossing and re-crossing the same stream
the comforting gurgle of water
always near
to the right or left

I didn't find you
but that was alright
far away, you are near
near, you are far away
while the path makes sense to itself
and leads me to this young rimu
green and weeping
among friends

MATARANGI

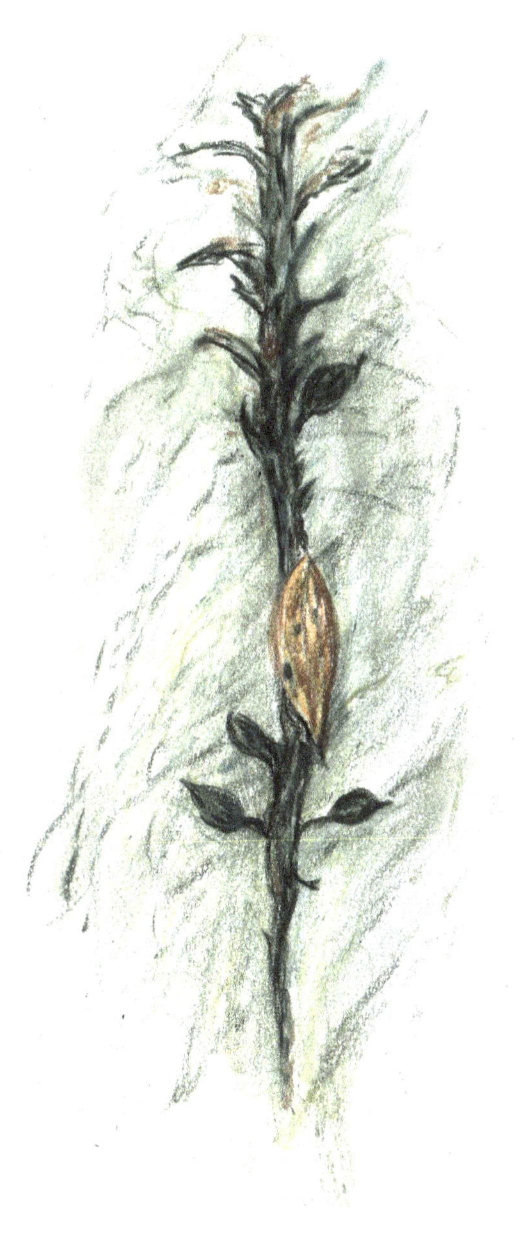

the blue drift

I sit by the rocks
out of sight of god
at the eastern end of the beach
fire up a dream
and vanish
into the blue drift

an old black-backed gull
eyes me with stern suspicion

we've arrived
but we have a long way to go

you head for the water
a step behind your reflection

soon we will settle our fates
and apportion our lives

at the world's edge
I puddle
through the shimmer and glitter

I could walk all the way
to next week's rain
and still not get very far

I step over
a strip of seaweed
decorated with a leaf
reluctant to disturb
its silence

a set of tracks in the sand
goes nowhere

you must remember, Linds
my old friend
how we cultivated
that raw
unturned thought
that couldn't sleep

we didn't quite grasp
that words are
just vapours of the heart

now, waves make their
play for the sand
distant dark hills hunker down
in their shadows
clouds thin
over a honey cake sky

you return from the water
a step ahead of your reflection
covered in stars

you look to the line
of holiday homes in their
spooky
immaculate emptiness

all this was once a vast wetland
you said
teeming with birds

the gull's had enough of me
and takes off
heading for the high blue
until it is nothing more
than a faint undulation of air

Coromandel wake up

let's wait
allow the water to cool
if it's going to cool

watch Coromandel wake up
to the day's heat haze
or become a dragon
under the reign of shadow

wait for waves to perfect themselves
on the shore

or for the family group
two adults three children
strolling along the water's edge
to grow old

wait for the bees to conclude
their fastidious love affair
with the lupin

and for a host of gulls to gather
out of an abundant past
to pick away at wet sea grass

forged

the mist folds over the hills like soft lips
blowing cool jazz

they call it a brooding sky
or a bruised sky, but the waves
have gone gentle after the storm
there's enough blue for a sun to show
and enough dark for another bout of rain

I am forged by this morning
gray as river rock
and remember the long, loose riverbeds
and the soft cry of their stones at night

there's a white line in the stillness
hair like wheat in the swirl of it
foam racing across the sand pushed
by devil winds

your job is to be a piece of dragon
half sunk in the sand
my job is to remember all
that can't be forgotten
in the age of forgetting

I don't know how to come out of the dream
how to make everything that is is
I'll let the pen run right off the edge of the
page
to write lines in the air
before I can hold you hard to my heart

there is no other direction for the eye to take
but over the bent line of the hill
no other words to describe the amorphous mist
the lowering sky, the run-on sand
the backward, leaf flipping
memory
of a bend in the river
and the thump of tractors

I never imagined, not once
that I would be here
that things would turn out like this
feeling hollowed by all we have done
to our one and only place
we've come a long way along
the banks of the Rakia River
down south

nothing else counts but blackberries
and pikelets, with cream
and silly talk of the intelligence
of a sparrow

I'm trying to make peace with it all
but that doesn't imply negotiation
I like to have faith in the world, too
some skin in the game
hot tea, a poached egg
(the sparrow on one leg)

I have to let the mind slide
as everywhere the light is raised

deadly grace

waves moving up the estuary
against the wind
flick back like silver fish
trying to take flight
while
the incoming tide is eating up the mudflats
faster
than I can write these lines

the mind can run as far as
the eye can see
and over the horizon line
where there be dragons
and the sudden
endless fall
of a wading white heron
its deadly grace
the backward flit of its leg
before moving forward
its power of concentration
and ability to create around itself
its own time zone
of stillness and calm
before the time comes
to strike

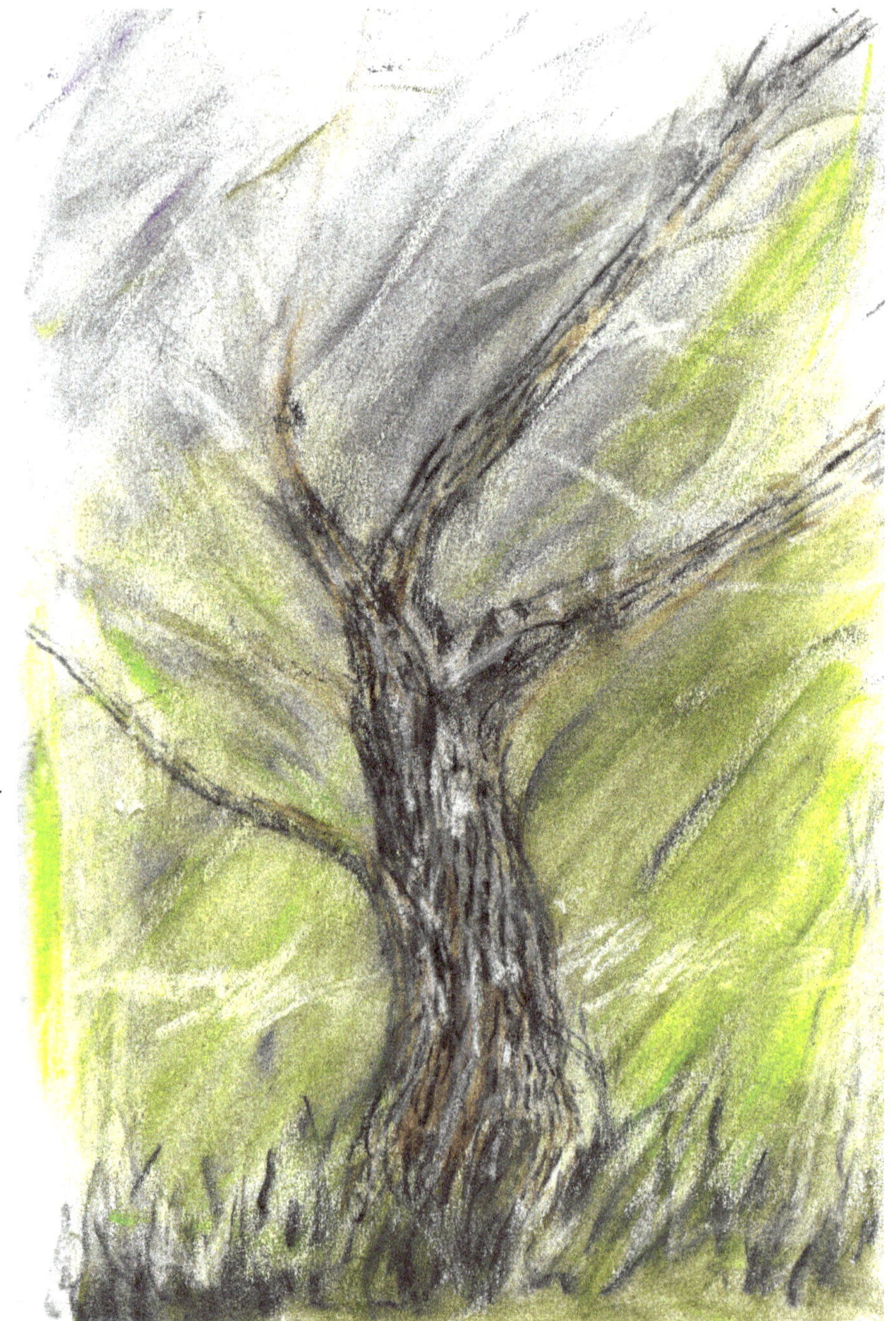

visit to Waikawau Bay

25

I lie beneath the ngaio tree
and look up at its flowers
hiding in the leaves like tiny white brides
you d hardly notice
and let the shadows criss-cross me

because there is nothing to do
I do nothing
so nothing gets left unfinished

with a pillow for my head
I don t envy the busy sparrow
always on the hop
or the vigilant hawk
forever turning
even against the sunset
behind a lattice work of poplars
or the mad skylark
its endless chitter

I think I know the language
But I haven t grasped the time signature

I wrap myself in the blue sky
as if it were a blanket
and close my eyes to the
sharp grass
(colours are the sufferings of light)

bird sketches

*

at dawn, the dotterel is a brief concurrence
of sand and light and wind
the ocean the colour of iced tea

*

too lazy to use the other
the oyster catcher hops around
on one leg
others bob their heads about
in a curious carousel motion
that may be their rites of spring
performed to the music of their bones

*

from here
the beach goes on
forever
into the western haze

gulls stand stiff against
falling silver

a piece of driftwood
gets up
and flies away

WHAKANEWHA

Waiheke Island

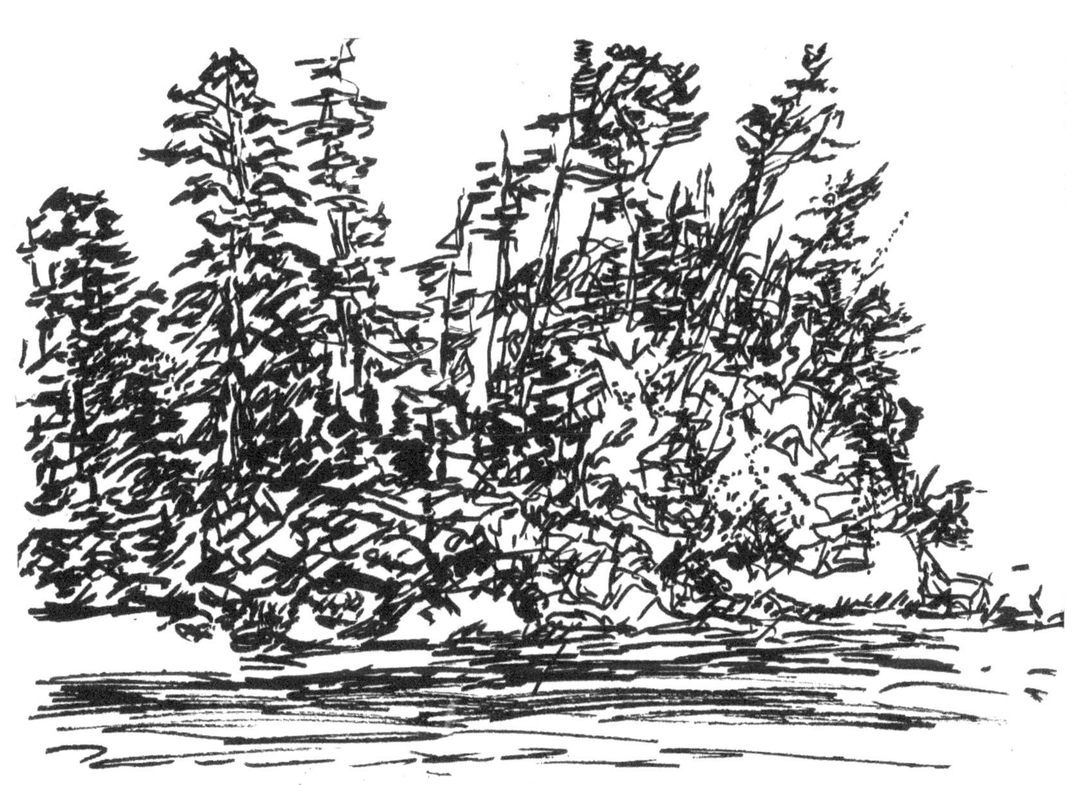

Whakanewha
New Years Eve 2019

we stand by the sign that says
no dogs allowed
and look out towards the low tide

from this distance the reeds and grasses
look as soft as a painter's brush
flax stalks make hieroglyphics
against the sky's backwash

you wander off to where the dotterels live
sketchbook in hand
everywhere you are you carry with you
and draw the rest from memory

far off, there's somebody under a pōhutukawa
embracing their shadow

in the soft wash of a muted
chrome haze
from the Sydney fires
the year's sun takes a rest
in a jumble of headlines

where mud meets the mangrove
in a burst of green and sullen yellow fruit
pied stilts make a run for it
in black and white and skinny red legs
but you need to look closer to see
the orange, burnt umber and red oxide
bubbling in the swamp

or the great flame erupting from the ocean
in a fit of white light

Whakanewha sunrise

It's comic the way the dotterels beetle along
the stiff, mechanical movement of their legs
their knees buried in the fluff of their bodies

this is their territory, their hour
their quietude, their place in the sun
their sky

the sea looks like silk, riding over
a hidden body, faintly ruffled
fragile

I remember you dancing at the funeral
your limbs were trying to escape from your torso
your voice had its own body
I didn't have a body, my limbs
were all imaginary

the flesh is still new
to the idea of bones
despite all the time in the world
to get used to it.

that which I once took for granted
now seems miraculous
and that which seemed astonishing
now looks ridiculous

I am gathered up in this one place
at least for the moment
we may have been here before
but never right now
and not even then

I deal in homeless lines and feckless rhymes
the door is open, the fish is on the skillet
the ferryman has been paid

there's always the flax to fall back on
a corner to sleep in
around the curve of the bay

sometimes the sea will rise up
to meet the light

with gestures quick and practiced
you catch
the rough stubble of the peninsular
the boatsheds of Rocky Bay
with all their history
and their new paint jobs

the caspian terns are
a quick sketch in flight
first light fends for itself
among the wiwi

the dead spent a lifetime
walking into the sun
there wasn't much left to bury

could we ever have moved
quiet and unseen
through the world
without leaving a crease?

we ride a fine edge
as the surfer shoots the tube

what is this, our little country
but a brief pause between eruptions.

journey

1
here we are

doesn't seem too far
uphill

you take the steps
steep steps ascending
I prefer the grassy verge

you disappear up ahead
I wait for you
to catch up with yourself

I can hear the balmy wind whispering something
about paradise island

2
at the top there is a picnic table
in a grassy patch
surrounded by trees

my thoughts are too scribbly for talk
and I envy the tiny warbler
who well knows its song

onward and upward
past the kumera pits
worn smooth by history
and hidden by kānuka

then down
to Whakanewha bay

where the tide is out
and on the ruddy brown and green
mudflat
seabirds perch on their own
shadowy doubles

3
in the distance
just before the line of
aquamarine
where the mudflat ends

a couple are calmly collecting cockles

Putiki Bay

across the ripple of the outgoing tide
heading towards the open sea
the late sun lights up Te Whau point
and gleams
on the windows of mansions
and streaks of white clay

an old boat shed leaning
towards the water
with the upthrusting bamboo
and the black, spiny wattle
puts me in mind of a Chinese garden
embroidered on a silk fan

I pick up a piece of driftwood
riddled by time
and greet my old friends from the north
Li Bai, Du Fu and Li He
drunkards of the word

comrades! let us raise a cup to the hour
and not ask, where is your country now
where are your hundred flowers?

look!
a kereru bellyflops out of a karaka tree
chased by spirits

the bare hills have turned tawny
for want of rain
see the ghost of the whau forest
all that's left is the name

suddenly
water begins to surge and gurgle
between the rocks
with no apparent cause

must be the ferry, I tell my comrades
passing around the corner of the world
just out of sight

then we see it, and laugh
and drink, and shout with glee
as it noses through
white puffy clouds

Putiki Point

(On hearing Leila Lees read her poem, Ferry
Crossing)

ferry glimpses of the past
one wave at a time
one pencil line
after another
light, faint and nerveless

when the sun appears
white caps turns silver
while the voices of our ancestors
recede
like an island fading to a speck

in your voice I hear
the generations of women
the westerlies they face
in their homes under the sea
the dip, glide and shudder
of their flesh
the forgetfulness of history

I see those women in their lonely
settler lives, their sky windows
their rough beds
the shadows in the corner of their eyes
their wandering deaths

and when you finish reading
your voice folds under the wake
bright and pearly in water colours

the power of the eagle

feels easy, lying on our backs
staring up at the clouds
bunched and dark
approaching from the north

the peaks of Rangitoto show
behind the hills of Anzac Bay
blue and grey
with a touch of purple

but nothing is that easy, really
only the words

nearby, a kawakawa wilts
from excessive spray
it's all devastation on the vulnerable
forest floor — the devas have fled
it's too quiet

you finish your sketch
and take out your brush
your water colours trickle into the bay
as the tide comes in

I want to take refuge in the ordinary
but it's not that easy to find
a face forms in the sky but it doesn't hold
long enough to show you

you say, 'if you go to the top of Putiki O Kahu
you will meet the power of the eagle'

it's a long climb

drought

the tide was so far out
it was just a memory

the estuary turns into a landscape
of corrugated runnels of sand
meandering streams
and sea-grass lakes

the bay is a water-colourist dream
of merging textures and emerging tints
from red to grey and grey to green
shadows
sneaking around pools of light

'Don't walk on eggshells'
the sign pleads
dotterels need their space

the shiny flax gleams and twists
as the late light shoots the gap

the sky is like an eggshell
light blue and airy, faintly speckled

we need space too
even these rough, windblown spaces
a comforting sense of largeness
and distance from everything

the world wears its mask of fear
but there's nobody near
just you and me
a mere stone's throw from
some understanding

'There's a cyclone coming tomorrow'
you say, as we head for Dotties Lane
'let's hope it will bring rain'

nice to feel upbeat
here in the downwind
with the caprosmas dying
the tairere dying
even the mighty mahoe
looks sad

but the tide has at last turned
and nobody knows just what will fill the world

on the cascades track

the track curls and dips
opens out
cross-hatched with light
backlit with shade

there're slender kānuka, sky high
the knotty mānuka
with its rough, flakey trunk
as we descend
into the gloom of the nīkau grove
the haunted green of the nīkau grove
where the years keep pushing up
into the sky

see the patupaiarehe
a mere flick of a green tongue
across a random patch of light
caught only
out of the corner of the eye

this is no closed-room silence
or the oppressive quiet of absence
but open-ended and borderless
lit by the silver darts of tūī's song
and the glittering jabber of the skylark

and here we are — don't know if
we'll make it to the cascades
but we might make it back
to some known road
if the track stays true

on the return I pause to write
'when in the light
I seek the shade

when in the shade
I seek the light'

nikau grove

we have been here before
and before that
and even before that
before these long, spindly trees
ever grew
and humans were unthought of
no ground dreamt them
no wings touched them

these palms collect their years
in rings on their trunks
and memories in their seeds
the silence speaks of changes
we can't unwind
tears that were never shed
sorrows that shrank back into themselves
and mossed over
these small hard kernals
lit in the crossfire of mind

look, my love, see
the way they lean upon each other
lean on their shadows
as their shadows grow richer
the ages pile up, time's squishy sediment

when they fall they make a bridge
not only across that boggy stream
but to the cry of the tui
the sudden flight of the ruru
the unspun dark
the unshed tears
a bridge from here to there
if not back again

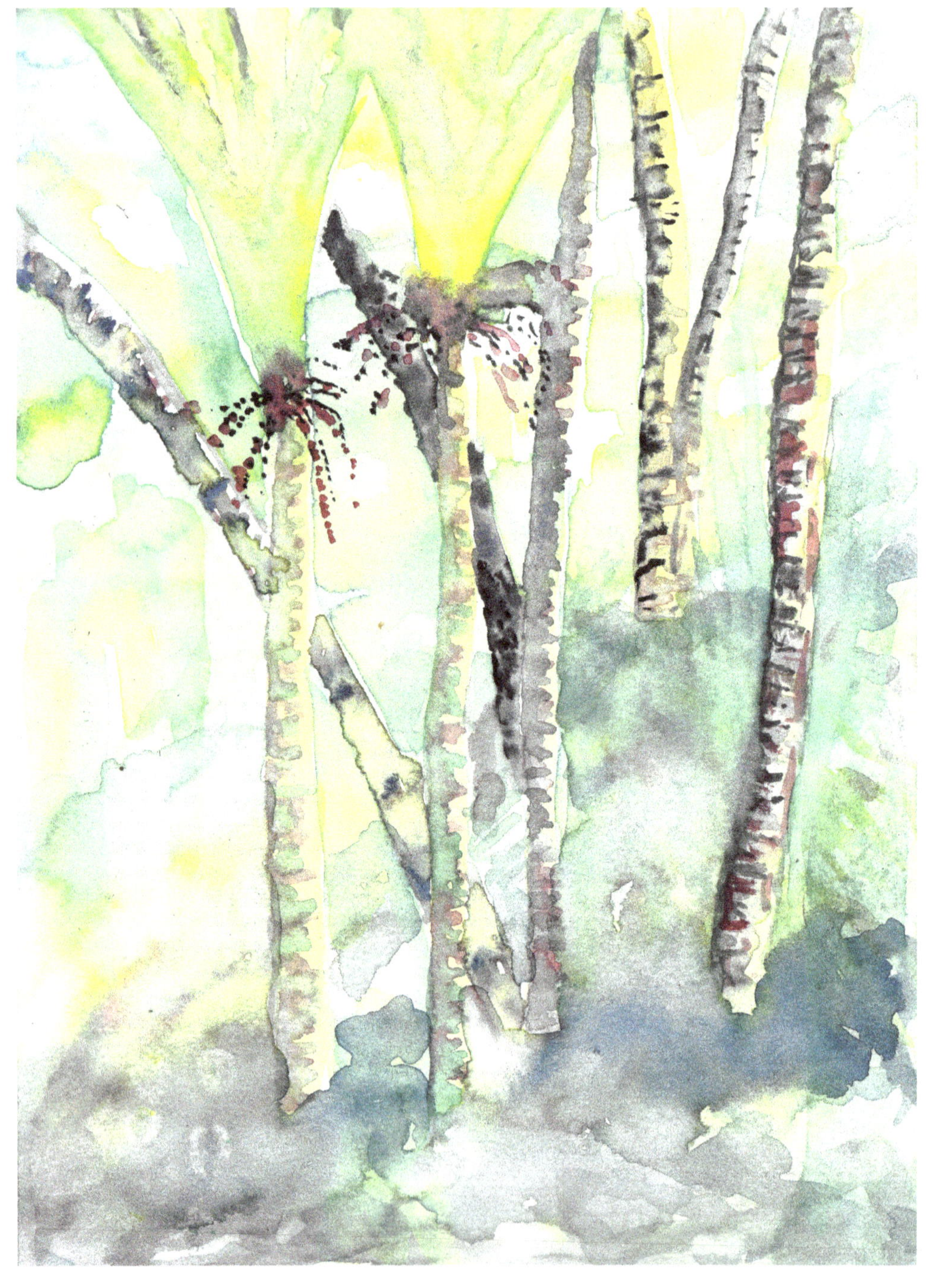

I allow the silence to rest in my ears
like a sleeping baby
to open interior distances
between me and my years
to listen to the beat of green
the voices of mingled light
and be with the nikau
in their motionless flight

dotterel

stiff-legged
leaning to one side
one wing bent
emitting helpless cries
moving in half circles

the dotterel leads us away
from its nest

the sand is peppered
with its tiny prints

somewhere, in the other direction
in the warm sand
a tiny spaceship
prepares for landing

standing on Whakanewha beach looking north

everything is so still I can hear myself think
hear a bird call from the other side of the sky

the sea is flat enough to walk upon
it hardly fragments
the shape of the sky

best the day not progress too fast
everything is just right as it is

the crunch of my boots on the sand
is enough of a racket
enough to alert the world

a white mushroom glows
with its own strength

soon the air will charge up
to the sound of engines
waves will take to the shore
while an offshore breeze will see the ocean
ripple and slide

fantails will arrive to make a home in my hat
we'll share a twittering moment

two ducks will fly up a bathroom wall
of the most steadfast blue
and I won't be standing here anymore
sketchbook in hand
but walking off somewhere else

crosslines

*

as you take a quick swim in the chill water
my eye scoots about
before settling on a raft of yachts
resting easy
on patches of white mist

*

the sea is hiding its voice
an old man nods into his memories

the sky does a wheelie
an empty pipi shell
a lone puff of cloud
where his ancestors went whaling

the sky is disturbingly free of signs
shouting to each other
the stories are empty
with their harpoon voices

*

a fisherman's rod flashes in the sun
a brief revealing
catching fast on the sky

that soft light is made of flesh
the silence is an hourglass of running sand

*

the kayaks arrow
through the slick light

hardly making a scratch
on the water

a heron raises its wings
and minces across the mud flat
a little wind stirs the air
beneath the pines

the nesting dotterel go quiet

ONETANGI

Waiheke Island

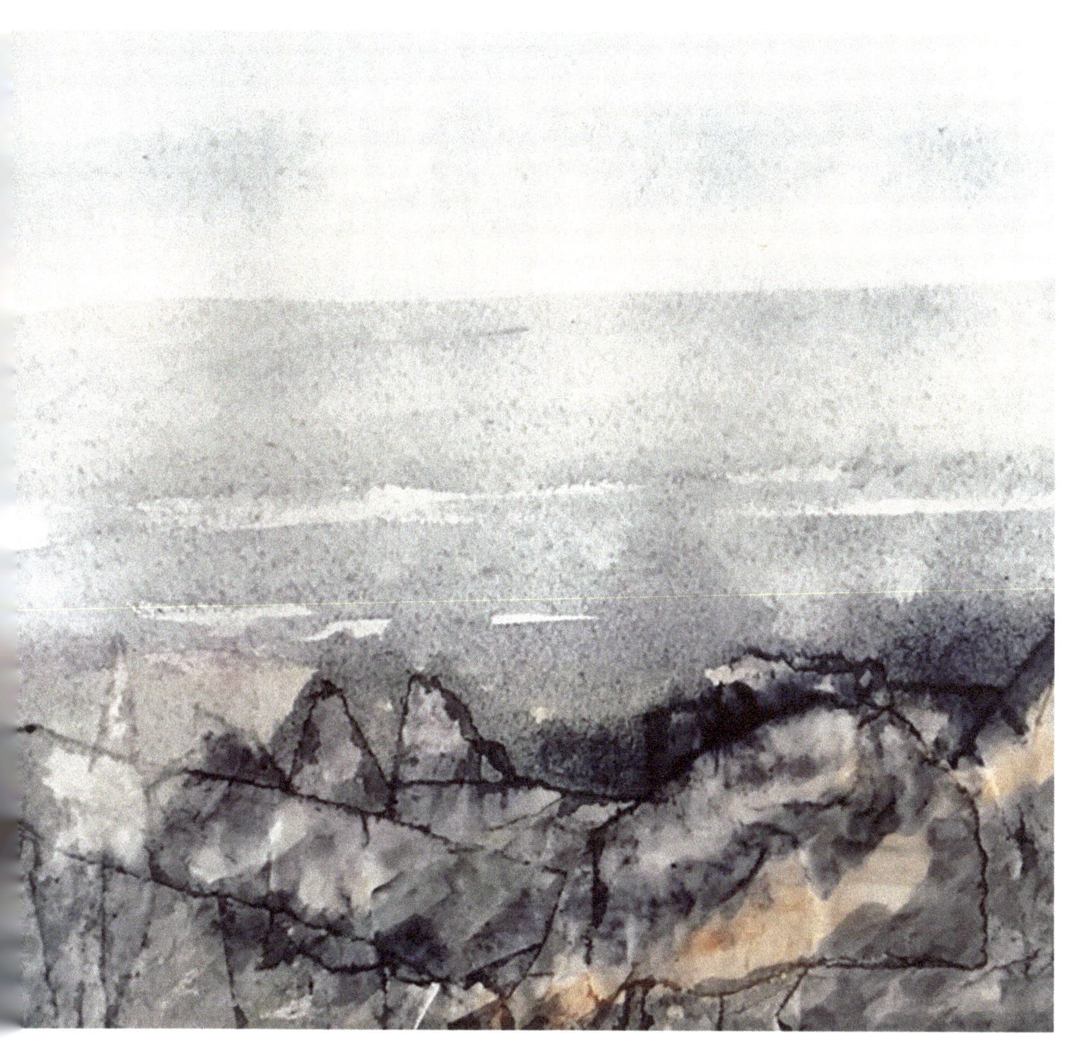

sunrise

I crave, the long, wide, open spaces
the warp, bend, curve of coastline

rain has pockmarked the sand
the pine trees show a rusty edge

people walk back and forth, in and out
of their isolation, with nowhere to go

they want to make new shapes
with their bodies, as the hills make

shapes with the sky
and white makes shapes with blue

here and there, geologies of feeling
does love ever go to waste?

this moment is another text
to an absent friend

the end is not far off
the road is walking backwards

as fast as it can
we have to hurry if we want to catch up

on Thompson's Point a small pine
leans at an impossible angle

small shift in configurations will push it
over

let's move into the sun where the sand's warm
make amends with the day

do our morning pages on the other side
of the night

in all this superlative stillness
a lone flax leaf keeps faith with the wind

we can think, but we can't not die
you have become adept with

textures, that's the word
perspective is an illusion

really, things just get smaller as you move
away from them

there comes a lightness
to the eye and the wind

the colour values keep changing
according to how we're feeling

you can't stop the movement of light
quickening on the hills, and on the skin

I'm sure it's the same for this sudden conclave
of oyster-catchers, their thoughts too swift

for us lumbering beasts to follow
it's a fat, waddling moment here on the sands

friend
where the end catches us all
by surprise

the horizon line

a set of footprints leads
from the sandhills to the sea

light follows them
along the shore line
agile on its feet

a splash of shadow
fills each print
with mind and memory

hills and mountains appear
out of nowhere at all
conjouring a sky

the ocean, in its living form
swallows everything up

these footprints I find
exactly fit mine, and lead
to the very edge of the water

where I stand
with nothing behind
and nothing before

but a tipping horizon
line

beach walk

it wasn't like that
the way it sounds

nothing out of the ordinary happened

my hat stayed on my head
you kept your council
and no one else came by

even the dog walkers stayed away

there was a pile of burnt sticks
where someone had made a fire

detritus along the grass line
from the last storm surge

a wet, bare expanse
left by the ebbing tide

I took off my shoes and numbed my feet
in the waves
nobody was swimming

I thought I heard someone speak
but when I turned around
I was the only one there

you were far off, by the rocks
lifting the sky into place
with a piece of charcoal

little waves

there are no pathways across
this expanse of wet sand
your feet can go anywhere
in any direction
with no particular intention
and hardly leave an imprint

the wind is light and airy
from so much open sky
the breath of the hills comes easy

there's somebody up ahead
but you're not likely to meet them
they'll be out of sight soon

here I am, high above my body
watching me walk
watching
little waves making soft sounds
against the land

Onetangi redux

there's not much to say
the world goes its way

a newsaper scatters to the four winds
nearby voices whirl about

an asian girl dressed in black
thows her cellphone into the sea

a dog jumps for a frizbee
and catches the moon

surfers lean and sway
up comes the seventh wave

I want to mention the sea grass
but it just lies about in clumps

inside the sand there are tiny insects
hopping from world to world

far cry

on a misty morning
the beach drifts off into deep time
and dream space

your texts from Frankfurt
do the same

here, human forms are rarefied
waves lap on another shore

that rumble
will be the morning flight to Vancouver
through clouds of gold

a large black-backed gull
hops in and out of frame
carrying the old moon

I throw streamers in the air
covered with words
but none find you

I walk my shadow home

ear to the sand

the forests of Gondwanaland
sigh
as the earth shifts
and trees remember the ocean

the night has a space to fill
high tide marks the horizon
every leaf a wave
every coastline
a memory

in the night sky
cities of the dead blossom and fade
a match lights up the dark
someone plays a guitar
the land exhales

the sandcastle melts away
before the incoming tide
until it is nothing more than
a lump of water

a starfish makes a bid for eternity
amid a great confusion of feeling

far off, the sound of children laughing
but I can't see them

I lie with my ear to the sand
and remember a continent

DEAD DOG BAY

Waiheke Island

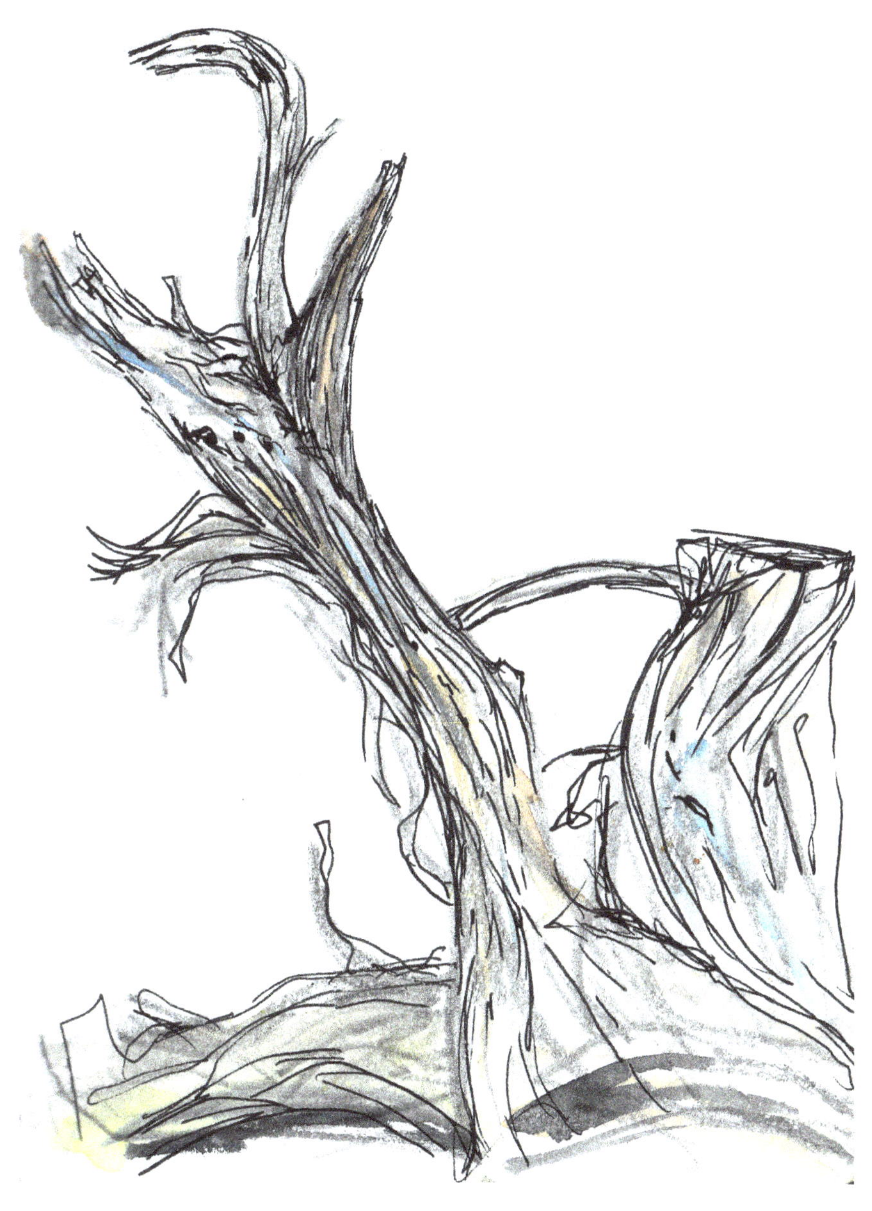

alone/together

1

we walk together
yet alone
we talk but we don't

a faint ripple on the dark lagoon
as we pass, like shadows

the silence is bigger than us
bigger than words
except for the sound of a distant motor
(there's always a motor somewhere)
and the greysong of mist

2

creeping sea levels have played havoc
with the coast
a pine tipped head first down a bank
roots of pōhutukawa meshing with thin air
as the clay falls away behind

a grassy verge made ragged by the tides

the ocean shifts uneasily against the land
contrary waves chop back and forth
to shifting winds
dreams get let loose and fly about
like real things

3

you sketch a stranded tree trunk
rising up out of the mud
stripped bare and white as marble

but you rough it in black

I wander off to visit a young mangrove
still learning how to breathe
and look across to Putiki

at the other end of the beach
you have vanished into the landscape
just another hunch of colour

I seem to have come all this way
from coast to coast
to understand nothing

far off

if you go away you might never come back
only the tide
has a good reason to return

few among us get so moon-struck

I walk along the low tide mark
everything waits
the world waits
a few thin-lipped waves
slap and gurgle

then I see you, far off
a walking shadow
and I can't tell if you
are approaching
or walking the other way

low tide

there's a special laziness
at low tide
a beat
a pause
a momentary suspension
a brief parity

the wings of the
white-faced heron
on the rise

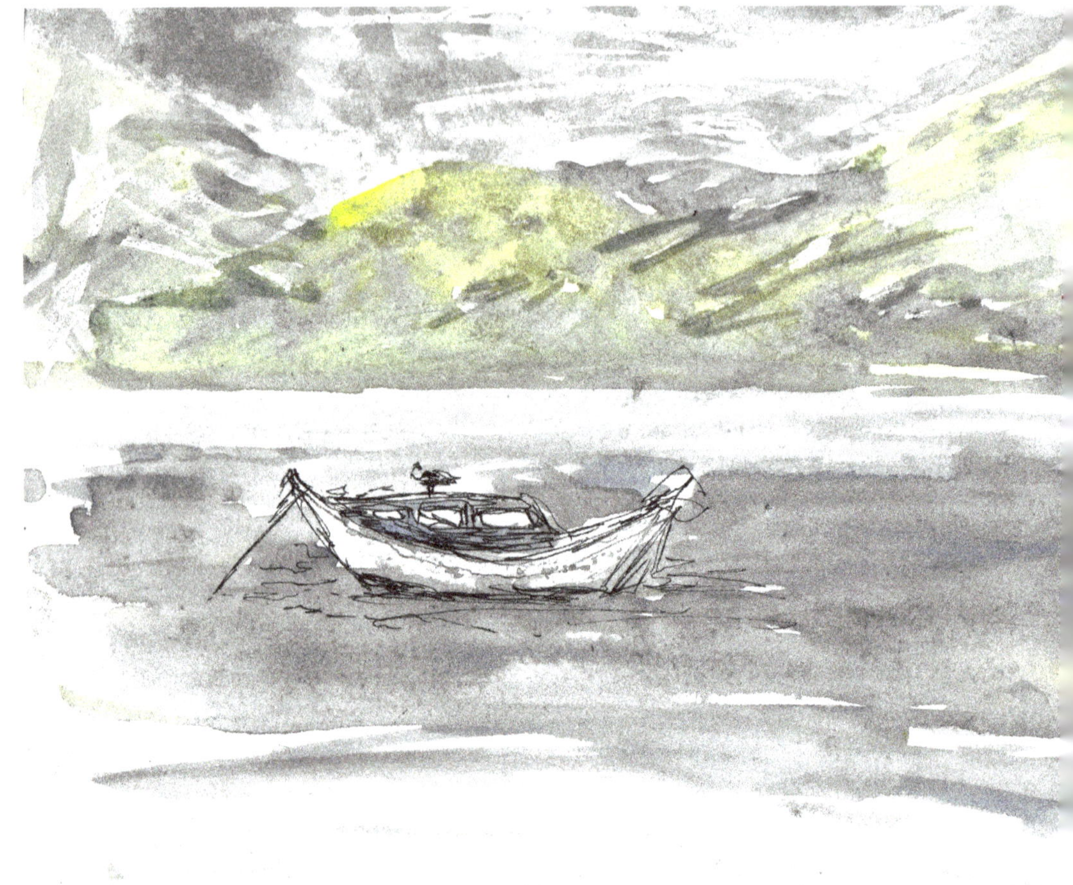

feel so lucky
as I was drawing/sketching.
a large stingray came
close into the shore.

Putiki Bay.

dinner

the cormorant smacks the water
in one clean dive
and
for a few
breathtaking
moments

turns into a fish
to catch a fish

then breaks the surface
beak first
turning
back
into a bird again

to sample the skies
and eat in mid-air

movement

the old path's been washed away
and leads to
a tangle of pōhutukawa roots

the rising sea has sculptured
caves of clay
where gnarly creatures live

here comes the sun
on the back of a seagull's wing

voices from all over
echo across the water
the sad tale of humankind

the death of things makes for
a special quiet
thought overlies it all

it was never meant to be definitive
never meant to show more
than a face

we sit on the damp sand
not caring about the cold
seeping up through our history

the terns sit quietly
like flecks of light
riding the wave

you could make a Ming vase
out the sky

the shape I mean
the long curve of a life lived
to reach this point

your cellphone lies on the sand
its black face blank
we can't be reached
but for those tangled roots
deep in fantasy

who can we count upon
we keep asking

goodbye Fyodor, goodbye Virginia
Dante has a special heaven sorted for us
where ancient harmonies rule
and the envelope of consciousness
is as fragrant as lavender

the gull turns down my invitation to dance
but that's alright
I didn't mean it anyway

I'm happy enough waiting
for the trees to release the sky
cloud stripped
and send us all reeling

the ruru doesn't cry much
beyond the dawn

it's all about movement, you say
the pen makes its mark
and there's no rubbing it out

PALM BEACH

Waiheke Island

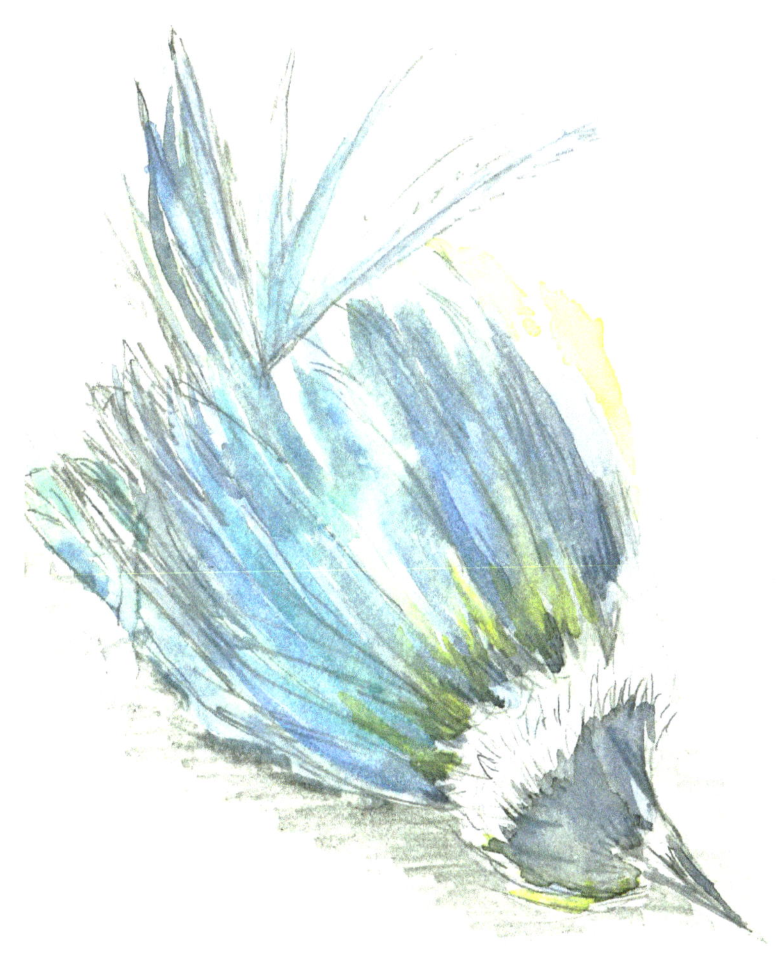

Dawn walk to Māwhitipana (Palm Beach)

we're early enough to catch the moon
still holding night in its yellow halo
the dead are held in tender care

we chuff along beneath the overhanging
tairere of Crescent Road
holding hands

Ngāti Paoa warriors pad along beside us
also heading for the beach
where they will fall, under the same moon
to invaders from the north

we follow that track
until history divides us

at the beach, the rocks are still
jagged shadows
sticking out of the water
while Coromandel gets a rosy tint

on steep slopes behind us
the toi-toi carries the flame

plovers circle
with their pterodactyl cries

I can see it! the long white cloud
stretching all the way to Whangaparoa

while you go for a swim, I draw
circles and stars
on the unblemished sand

from a distance

gulls float above the hills
like embers of light
flaring

there must be a dawn somewhere
in the making
must be a glad day
somewhere shaping

the sky is as clear as jazz
all the way to andromeda

the quiet beach waits
for the next wave

and here we are
living our own uncertain lines
in our frail houses
still learning to read

waiting for the rain to come

looking down at Matapana

off you go, down the track
your figure receding

the days have pulled in
the air grows chill

but no rain
even in prospect
except the memory of it
carried in the sky

sometimes, you don't know
there has been a storm
until the calm

across the dark grey sea
the silver streak of a ocean liner
hovering

the light is frail, I know
the sand will be cool
between your toes

on the peninsular
pine trees stand stiff
waiting their moment

you have reached the bottom
of the track now
one more turn and you will vanish
into the rest of your life
sketchbook in hand

soon there will be nothing left
but a few lines
and a charcoal smudge

every goodbye can feel
like the last goodbye

shingle crunches underfoot
as I walk away

I'm not up to it today
I feel invisible
no one can see me
everybody looks past me
the clouds pass through me
without a sound

words are felt
heavy in the body
dogs mock their chains

as the world comes to life
blue streaks blue, green
streaks green
with roads and houses
in between

nearby, a morning radio plays
some crying song
from long ago

the beginning

Hauturu Island
a resting place for errant breezes
is raised up
upon a layer of mist
and an indefinate horizon

this early haze is soft on the gaze

just offshore
a man sits in his fishing boat

there's a cave between the rocks
where shadows live

there are a lot of memories here
scampering around on little legs

a womans stands under her hat
and lets her eyes ride seaward

if you lie on the sand
with your eyes closed
you will be, once more
at the beginning of the world

Little Barrier Islands, Palm Beach

faint lines

after a while
there's always a wave behind
overtaking the one in front

kyaks red and green
are pulled well clear

like J Afred Prufrock, I wear
my trousers rolled
and go for a stroll

the sand is still warm
from the day's heat
shadows are growing feathers

Rakino is passing
into the light

there will be time, there will be time
'I think I'll draw the bunny-grass' you say

up ahead, a man in a black hat who's not me
walking the dog
makes me wonder who I am
and who shows me the steps to take
along the tide line
where little pools of darkness gather

a couple walk hand-in-hand
no finer sight
her dark hair far down her back
his shadow grows ambitious

everything's getting luminious
the scattered kelp lies about
like creatures from the deep
about to lift off from their gleaming tarmac

gulls circle you where you kneel, drawing
faint lines

the picture postcard perfect
poem

I mean, it's all so tranquil
so much spark and sparkle
like a fresh apple in a picnic basket
like a carefully cropped poodle
like a sweating bottle of champagne
so insufferably fresh

that puffy silver cloud, very obliging
with no dark lining
the pōhutukawa glowing red
as advertised
hang lusciously over the water
when the tide is in

there's milky foam on wet sand
the ocean turquoise of course
(what other colour, darling?
aquamarine might be a contender)
and cool and clean
with vibrating depths and
David Hockney style refractions

here young people frolic   a man
the perfect idol with rippling abs
a woman with a black hat, a white top
and smooth brown legs, so stylish
walk past a gleaming fizz boat
that ferry people and poodles in
from bobbing yachts, also gleaming

others drape themselves across
brightly coloured towels

resting easy

I come here
to put down anchor

the hills around
don't move too much

at high tide
the bay stretches into light

there is comfort here
where me and my craft
might rest easy

the waves come and go
beneath, to beach in lines of foam
quite happily

I like the sound the anchor makes
as it rattles into the depths
seeking purchase
and the way the sails roll up
like secret scrolls

and, for the moment at least
there is no destination

ONEROA

Waiheke Island

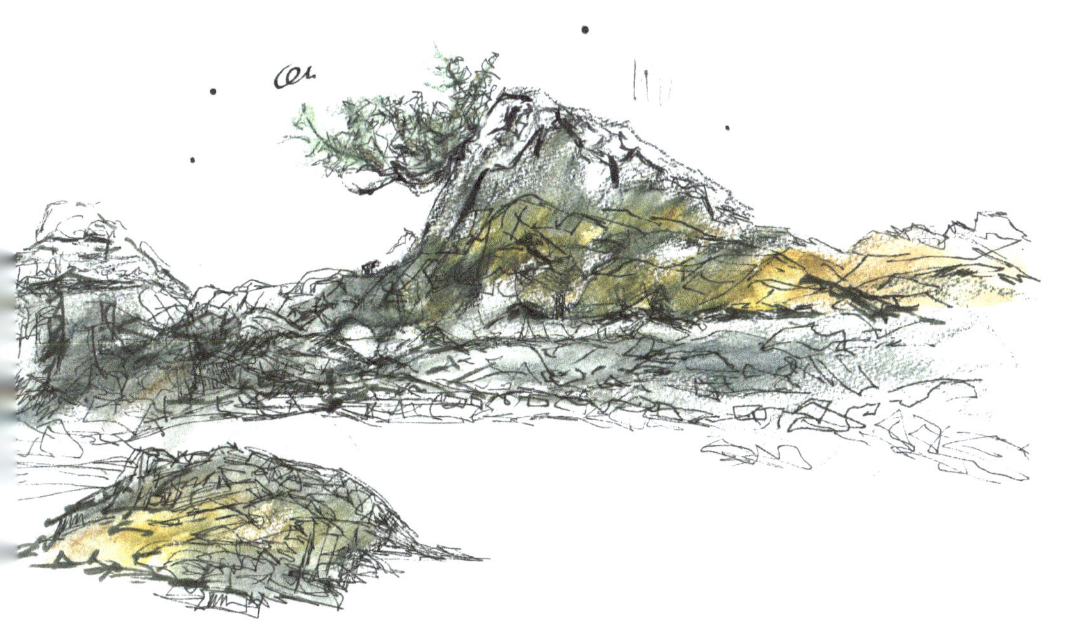

nouns turn to verbs

nouns are just slow verbs
I think you said
the horizon line is never straight
we just see it that way

Coromandel looks ethereal this morning
like some far off Tolkien land
where orcs come pouring out of the mist
I'll prose them down with some hot words
and pour verses on their graves
for a special treat

the sky has been done with a careless hand
while seagulls the size of horses
peck children off the sand

summer's barely come and it's gone
just like that

there are three moons in the sky
one for me, one for you and
one for the pot

moon rocks crawl up and down the beach
and dissolve into slow sand

make tea best with water that is
chuckling

the dog walkers leave the beach at ten
and the world returns to form
nouns are verbs in disguise
I thought you said
a tall sky gathers the wind

Owhanake

I like the way you take off your shoes
to better feel the mud squishing up
between your toes
and walk it, humming
a kiddy's song

I'm not prepared for the steep steps
that take us up and around and back
and along

the walk wearies me
body's gone to pack
have to go slow
like some old geezer
a donkey under a load of years
and don't want to be caught out here
naked and crumbling
like these cliff edges

I'm not as smart as the little mānuka
that has learned how to lean away
from the wind
and hoard its fire in its pith

I pause
pretending to enjoy
the tumble of sea sounds in my ear
and the clouds over Rakino
like beaten egg-white
and the mansions on the hillside
full of wealth and pride
while I catch my breath
the only breath I've got
which doesn't want to be caught

we were here before, you and I
it feels like that
we've lain in this same patch of grass
for many a lifetime
as I followed my pen to the edge of the page
and back again
and you painted the scene
with your eyes, over and over
until all the colours shone

you show me the slender ake ake
with its sticky sheen and
where the tūī hides
among the karo tree's tiny red flowers
searching for nectar

from this height, it all looks quiet
almost serene
Rakino on the horizon
a slice of green
the ocean a standing wave

I remember my mother teaching me to say
aroundtheruggedrockstheraggedrascalran
and to do it fast
I have to laugh
I never could get it right
but I don't have to lean
too far
or fly
to see the rugged rocks
in the roiling rivers
down there
in the shadow of the hill
we're standing upon

looking west

you come to this little cove to sketch
a tree in the throes of the sky

I'm here for the upswing
of a pogo stick morning, fresh
as a cut lily
but all I can see
is
the holy river of the Ganges
swollen with bodies
the air thick
with the smell of corpses
and the blood of dead children in Gaza
flowing as soft as a lullaby into the sand
and I can't think straight anymore
can't hold thought upright
can't maintain
a clear heart

I resist everything that is blue
the lighness of my own step
resent my facile content
my eye, always seeking beauty
even in the dark torment of rock

I don't want to stick out
of the side of the world
like that bit of tree
hanging onto nothing

you can see lots of houses from here
the Oneroa dress circle it's called
the self-important ones and

the outclassed ones
and those looking a little worse for wear
with not a drop of blood showing

ah, see, the tide always runs
with the wind
the yachts find their center of gravity
around their masts

me, I stumble on the path
back up into our lives
and eggs benedict at the Wai Caf

meanwhile, as I transcribe these notes
the morning after
a thrush outside my window
has never stopped singing

PIHA

'By the same road to the same
sea, in the same two minds
to run the last mile blind or
save it for later.'
(Alan Curnow)

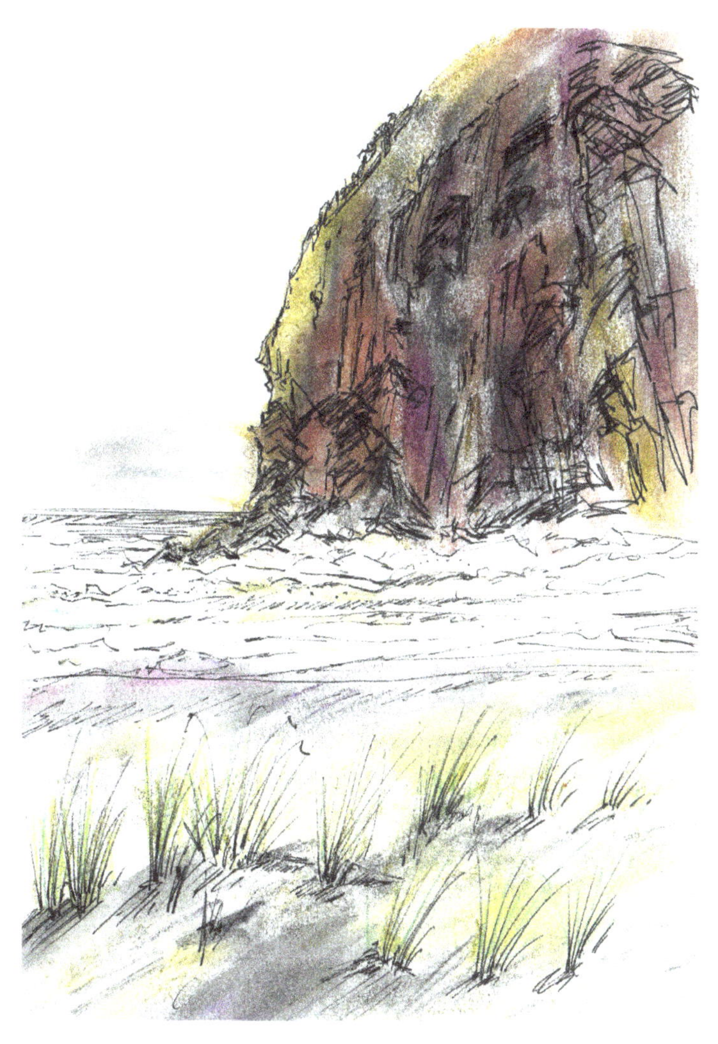

Lion Rock

in a great fury/the gods hurled these rocks/down onto
the black sand/from some far distant cosmos/and never
came back/to clean up/now they are barely covered/in
light green fur/waiting to grow from their hard roots to
the tumbrel sky/and for the clouds to tickle their most
inaccessible places/walking, it is possible to imagine/
that there never were any people/ever/ but only slow time
to batter and hollow and eat into their stony souls/black
beetles in their crevices/they are chipped away by bird
song and rough Tasman winds

lines of light open into a circle

here, we need to remember/that the ocean is the mother/
womb of all quickening things/and we may be dead before
the tide turns/sheer hillsides no chains can hold them
this whenua steeped in their wairua/love and flax/green
is the nicest haunting

Wai O Kahu

I always feel safe around running water
the way it comes into time and out again
as if dimensions were no problem
moss is the mercy of stones

a curved path pleaseth the eye
the end
is always just up
around the next bend
carry me legs
carry me
find the kauri
surface as pitted as the moon

and onwards, I wanted to be
near the sound of falling water
to feel the stone hillside at my back
to full and glisten there
the deepest part of the waterfall
where the mystery is greatest
and I know myself to be
a creature of that mostness

leaning towards the land

too big for the eye
on the halloween glitter
of black sands

this rock is no sketch
'hills don't have colours like that'
I say, but I wasn't looking hard enough
let the line fall

after applying the colours
you paint with the wet ends
of your fingers
then pen and ink for the pubic spaces

a couple of black-backed gulls
settle down to await eternity
and keep an eye on us

it gives pleasure to give pleasure
we can leave it at that
let me be like the everlasting
drawing, like a tall rock
leaning towards the land

surely it was never this light and airy
where are we actually?
in the surf's slow over-arm
I breath and I am alive
tihei mauri ora

Interiors

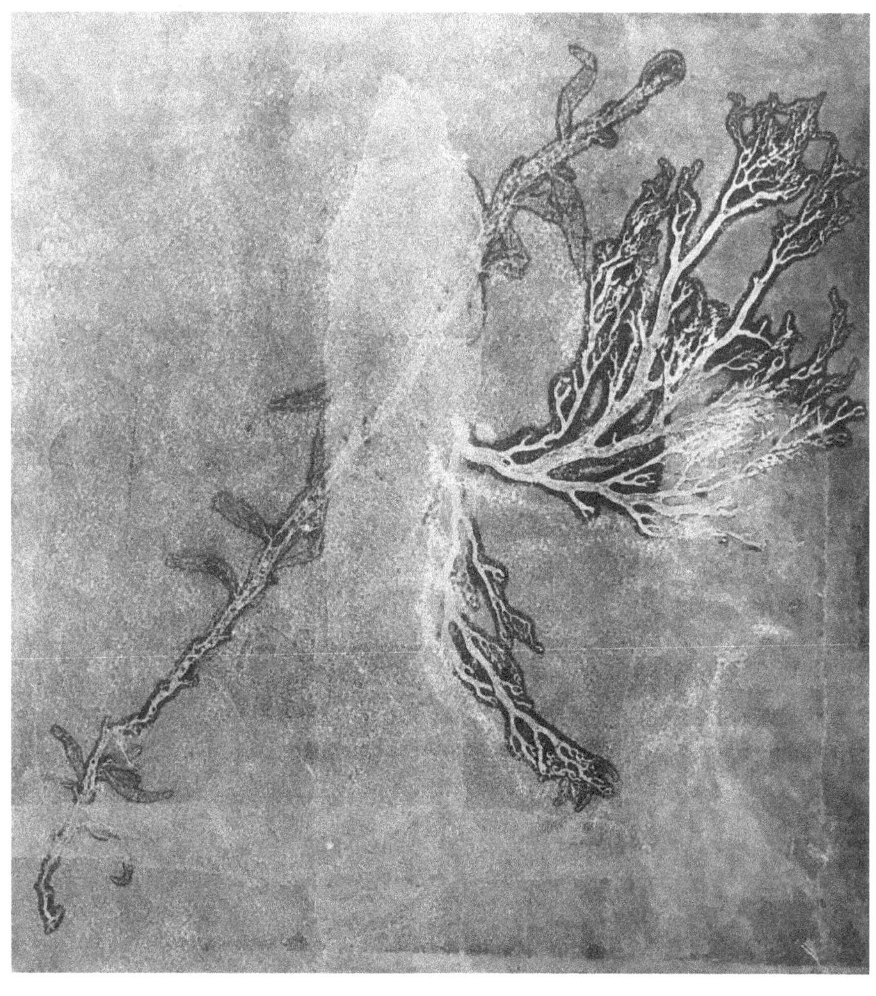

THE PAST

Forever is composed of nows

(Emily Dickinson)

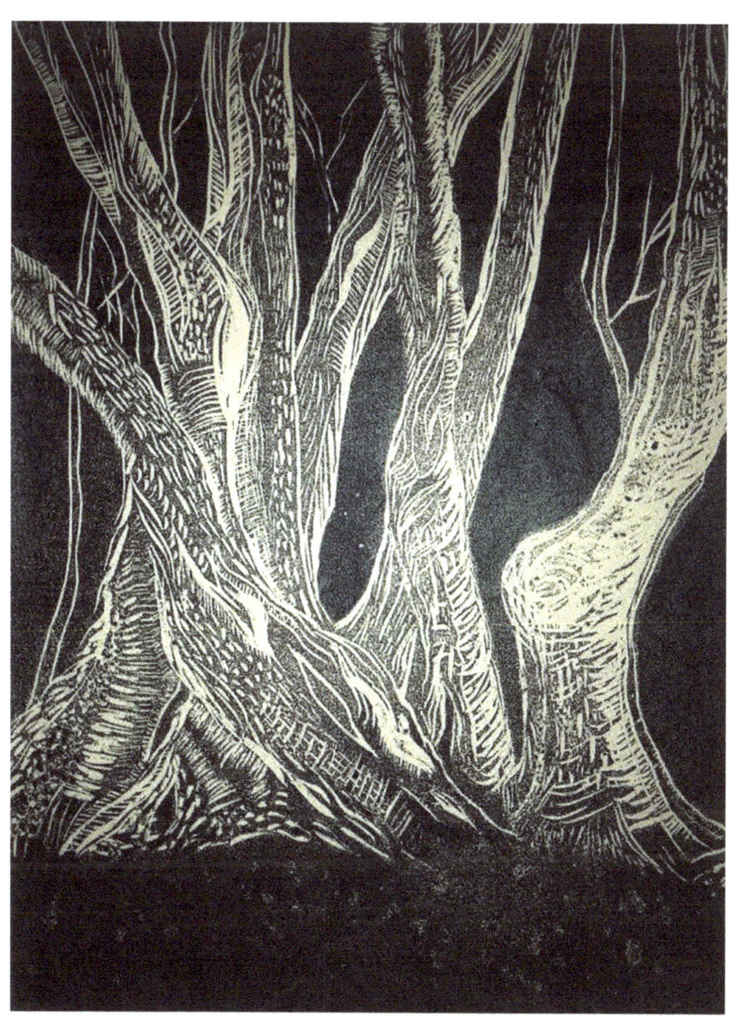

for Anna Akhmatova

this past century
what a riot
dazed and confused
it touches the fever
for which there is no vaccine

summer's sun still lights up the north
houses settle into the earth
their antennae strain towards heaven
hawks circling in, hawks circling out

Anzac 2020

no dawn parade and no rain
people stand stiff by their letterboxes

there's something primeval
about dawn
the eternal light that gathers
behind the hill
turning trees into silhouettes
pouring shadows into the
flowering shapes of
negative space

the sky that fits those dark shapes
is at first red, then eggshell blue
then thunders into light
as death goes about its way

and the hushed voices
lest we forget

the past

there is my mother
bending over herself
there is my father
who turns into a spade
sticking up out of the potato patch
there is the familiar sky
aired
and neatly folded in the linen cupboard

there are the regions of childhood
discarded in the toybox

once there was a pond
and a boy who courted dragonfly moments
sailed rough boats
he made himself
and learned how hard it is to kill an eel
without a gun or axe

the past is not smooth
like the icing of a cake
but lumpy
forming
layer after layer of instants
and sidereal years
lived
and unlived
moments trapped in swamp gum
made amber and eternal
in sepia prints
where everyone's skin is smooth
and everyone is facing the camera

you pry apart memory's sealed lips
for the hidden pearl
and feel inside
for the smooth, slippery meat
and the scent of vinegar

we made our pact at the feast
with the juice still fragrant on our fingers
and our words were like tongues
still hot in our mouths

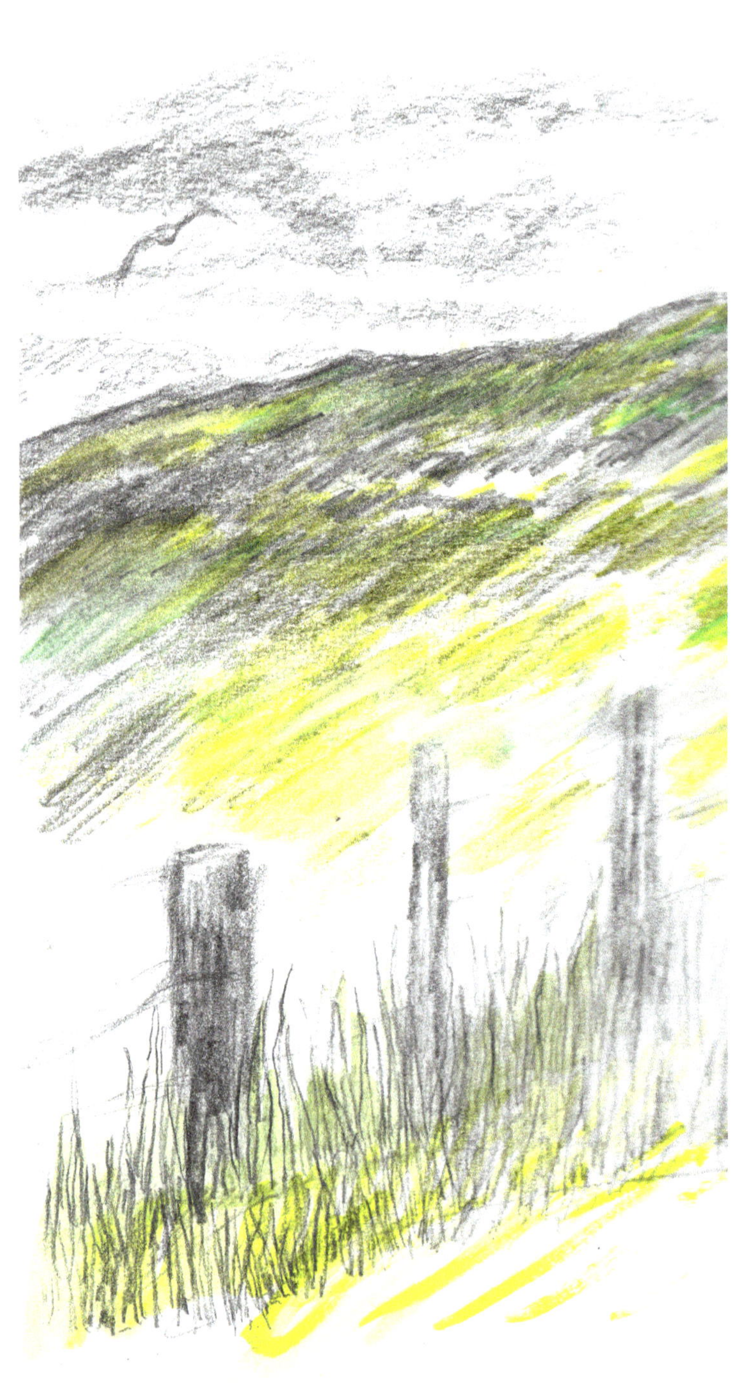

the photograph

the photograph of my father
discovers him

standing in a doorway
on the threshold of a life
he won't get to live

a joke he'll never catch
a jackpot that got away
a quinella that went bust
a war that came full circle

a hand-in-the-pocket moment

he will turn
leave his laugh at the door
and vanish into the shadows behind

and that joker with him
(what was his name again?)
will exit the right-hand frame
looking for a fresh drink

he'll find another person
and tell the same funny story

I want to take back
to recall
in the best sense of the word
every step that brought him
to that shuttered instant

everything snaps into focus
and it's too late to reconsider
the arrangement of light and shadow
distance, form
and the rule of three

too late to back away
the word is out
the moment cannot escape itself

too late
to be
elsewhere
in the cross-hairs of actuality
its cold epiphany
set against his warm mirth

the only evidence
that such a moment
ever existed

poem without a hat: for A J

Grandaughter A, (who's very nearly four
you know) and I
empty an old trunk to see what can be seen

we search among the bits and pieces
for the bits and piece lost between
the slow glass and the dream

scraps and facts and Max all in one trunk
a polished stone from Birdling's Flat
(I think there's a bird inside)
a withered kiss pretending to be
a squeezed lemon
an old analogue telephone that still hums
a jar of stars, you can shake them around
a seed from Africa, haunted red
dinosaur bits of deep time
scattered like lego

and this mounted photo of the Hinds Rugby Club
circa 1957, with me in it, (that's me
second in from the bottom right
I played on the wing, ran so fast
my feet hardly touched the ground, you know)

look, here's some dark clouds that forgot to rain
and a feather that fell out of the sky
on an ordinary day just like this
some forgotten couplets holding hands
somewhat forlorn
a metaphor that's had its day
a rhyme turned grey
but never fear, the poem is here

on this old yellow page
thrown away

there's everything here, except my hat
which doffed itself
but we go on searching just the same
for that's the way we play this game

Patch Pants the Tailor
(For George Christian)

As a kid I had a book written
in the year I was born
called Patch Pants the Tailor
who cut trousers from a blue sky
and a jacket from fluffy clouds

Patch Pants goes for a cosmic walk
across the original dawn
scissors in hand
while a couple of fishermen
head out into the Gulf
hoping for snapper

I park my mind in the shade
and let my words go for a walk
all by themselves
holding tight to Patch Pant's hand

kākā live in the Hekerua Valley
their cries harsher than salt
they are finely attuned to grief
the echo of the world
just over the horizon

two white-eyes flash by
in hot pursuit of each other

morning belongs to the birds
who can lift its light or catch
its spark

they fly off the page of child's book
where Patch Pants has learned
to patch the world
and so escape his poverty

my father blacked out under the weight
of a sack of sugar
Patch Pants sewed him a shroud

I watch you draw, the colours coming fast
built up in layers
the vanishing peninsular, the far flung
scribble, the tyranny of time and place
with a strip of pure texture
and Patch Pants the tailor
who dreams of freedom
riding the sky

The almond tree

the almond tree is in bloom
pink and white
and delicate
white and pink
and delicate
like a pretty white girl
like nursery wallpaper
like a book of rhymes
in the time of Mother Goose
under a sky too blue to be true

didn't your mother have an almond tree?
you ask
but I don't like to remember
because
all almond trees are my mother's almond tree
in the year she died
after the blossom had fallen
under a true blue sky
and turned the grass white and pink
pink and white

Thompson's Point

If, in the future, someone
tries to find this old wooden gate
with a view over grassy hills
I doubt they'll have much luck

that gate has the look of something
that won't last, that's already history

which opens from a farm track
which has turned into a road
into a farm which has turned into a
real estate development

the borderlines are marked
the earth movers have arrived
the first turf turned

like me, the gate is having a problem
with one of its hinges
we can just grow together
old, decrepit and unhinged
until big shiny things
take our place

for L L

the westerly wind arrives in gusts
hand-in-hand with remembrances
winter dreams
and ferry glimpses of the past
one wave at a time
one pencil line
after another
light, faint and nerveless

you read me your *Ferry Crossing*
as the waves race around the peninsular
your voice as soft as a hug
your words folding over in the wake
as if they have never been

when the sun appears
white caps turns silver
while the voices of our ancestors
recede
like an island fading to a speck

in *Ferry Crossing* I hear
the generations of women
the westerlies they face
in their homes under the sea
the dip, glide and shudder
of their flesh
the forgetfulness of history

but with your invocation of pen and ink
and the quiet magic of paper
I see those women in their lonely
settler lives, their sky windows
their rough beds
the shadows in the corner of their eyes

                         their wandering deaths
                and when you finish reading
                              I just want
                  to hear it all again

the taraire

we leave the headland track
and turn to the interior
to find
the particular tree you have to draw

the taraire has a story
locked in its height
its old man wrinkles
and its erect, plum-dark seeds

it has seen the best and the worst
and the unhinged years

there was a time
when they fired all the trees
just for the hell of it
stood back to admire their handiwork
as the world went up in flames

what couldn't be cut and pulped
was burned
the birds lost their songs
the people lost their way
their hearts turned to iron
and ashes

I lie back and watch dark clouds
stack up over the gulf

a south wind brings the smell of rain
and the taste of ice

the taraire stands

vast and serene
in a wasteland of asparagus weed

I rest my head against the trunk
listening to the memories
it draws up from the stony dark
down from skies of light
and hear the tree-rings singing
of the holocene

looking inland

you come to this little cove to sketch
a tree in the throes of the sky

I pop in out of a dream
just to be here for a while
all I can see
is
the holy river of the Ganges
swollen with bodies
the air thick
with the smell of corpses
the blood of dead children in Gaza
flowing as soft as a lullaby into the sand
and I can't think straight anymore
can't hold thought upright
can't maintain
a clear heart

I am smeared across the face
of too many years
with my fungal hopes
and running dreams
I resist everything that is blue
the lightness of my own step
resent my facile content
my eye, always seeking beauty
even in the torment of rock

I don't want to stick out
of the side of the world
like that bit of tree
hanging onto nothing
the skin of my life has cracked open
to pour forth gray river stones
and sorrows untold

meanwhile, as I transcribe these sketchbook notes
the morning after
a thrush outside my window
has never stopped singing

Matariki 2020

the day's as short
as the night is long
sleep is stretched
across history
and the newest moon

wakefulness goes on forever
heralding the dead
the arrival of the living
and the co-mingling of their songs

a little rain sweetens the air
a bit of a chill sweetens the skin
yesterday's last light
merely a memory
wood smoke in our clothes

it is said that Ranginui the sky father
maddened by grief
at his separation from Papatūānuku
his sweet earth
tore out his eyes
and threw them into the heavens
where they would rise up and sing
into the long, insufferable night

soon Matariki will arrive, little eyes
these eyes of god
that spike the heart through
with their far voices

star-bound kites
and hot air balloons
will arise
like tiny, fiery hopes
into the void

TONGARIRO
NATIONAL PARK

It's just one s l o w   step
          after the other
          'How long
          til I'm down?'
          (Hella Bauer)

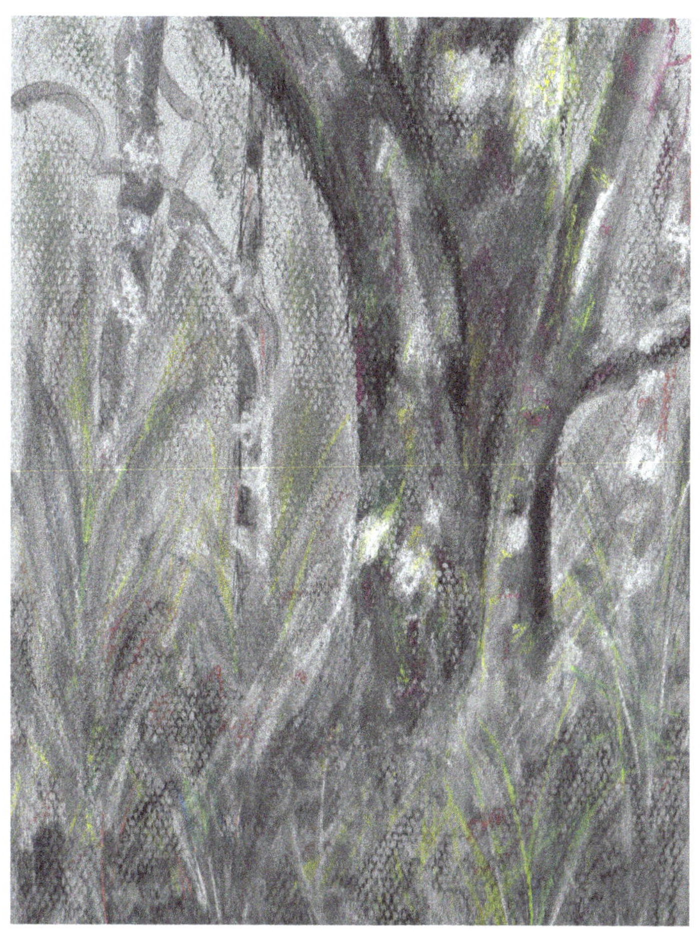

Ruapehu pieces

*

first the mountain is light
then it is movement
as we approach it moves
further away
by the time it arrives
I am gone

*

shadows fold and crease
better catch it now
you won't see its like again
not on this earth

all this open space reminds us of time
distance conjures the long chant of the land
the falcon's bleak cry

Ruapehu is dressed to kill
in a light lace of snow
a glimmer in clefts of rock
the mineral opera
in full throat

*

before the next snowflake falls
worlds will fall
into memory
and be clasped by rock

*

I've come all this way just to make myself
tired
in the tawny wilderness
pretending the last ten years never happened

only the shadows and the landscape beneath
are left to tell the story
to hide their form
the sky is deep within itself

*

three cries and
a skyline
I know the hawk by its lazy glide
the tītipounamu by its brevity

*

recite by candlelight and the words
will come for your soul

in that flame words will die
innumerable deaths
and we will smear the ashes on our faces

'first there is a mountain
then there is no mountain
then there is'

*

dawn discovers the mountain
in the palest pastels

they say there's trouble brewing in the crater
all looks sweet to me
but for a certain ponderous silence

the chaffinch, light and airy
is still around
to flirt with the light

along the mountain streams, the sleek stoat
still hunts for fresh-water cray

the kestrel still chases the quick-witted wax
eyes
between the shadows

a little rain still quickens rock pools

a wispy trace of cloud
vanishes in the moment

*

this point marks the furthest advance of the
lava flow
this Tolkienesque bunch of rocks is as far
as the magma could reach

here, it's all about shape and density

high up
with a deep valley either side

feels like a good place, I say
to witness an eruption

*

light can't be stopped
everything it touches, it frees

in a moment or two it will touch
this bench on which I'm sitting
and free me

*

I'm too close to death
to feel entirely comfortable

*

if I have to die
let it be with the sound of water
running through my head

all the wind would need to do
is close my eyes

*

since I'm in no hurry to get to where I'm going
it takes no time at all

we pause to discuss the colour of the tiny flowers
of the heather
are they white or touched with pink
is there mauve in there somewhere
or can they just recall
as a fragile memory
the russet red of leaves

*

it becomes all about light
    unalloyed light
    uncompromised light
    spacious light
in the uncluttered air
    bold or subtle
    overt or full of mystery
    flimsy or double-glazed

not in things but in light

Silica Rapids

*

I love to sit near the sound of running water
the Waikare River is my ally
the Waikare is my guide, my tipuna
the Waikare is a woman
all that rush and flow, that
mossy strength
creamy white silk

I am the river and the river is me

what a birth she has, rain and snow seeping
through cracks into the earth, down, down
to the hot volcanic heart of rock, then up, up
buoyed by heat, tracking along a fault line
enriched with silica and aluminium
bubbling to the surface
eager for the ecstasy of air

*

I lean back into Ruapehu
the red tussock is my bed
the burnt umber of the heather
reminds me of some ancient bloodline
the ageless rocks around are my mortality
the path below stretches off into the world

I close my eyes
and hear nothing but the Waikare
its fables and fixtures
the sky rushing past

*

last night I dreamed of the city
that I was lost in it
nothing was familiar
and all the people I knew
had slipped away

here I m home wherever I sit
everything is exactly in its place
where it fell

*

I'am
forever here
in the sky's encampment

I can talk to the man in the moon
for eternity, have his ear
alone, just as I am
with nothing but the wind
to answer to
I don't like to think
too much
thought holds no delight

memory is buried deep in the magma
in a community of beech trees
and in the marvelous clamour of the sky

Taranaki Falls

I wish I had more to give
I'm hung on the swift shadows made by the
water
as it passes ancient rock faces
and crowded dreams

I am the liberation of the wind
I am what holds me here
to stone and shadow
and gives birth to me in the icy pools
I approach, clambering over
the slippery ground wanting to
cry out
to get close enough to see
I don't know what
maybe a rainbow in the moss
the spirit of lava, andesite and silica
that eruptive rock
or secret fungal kingdoms
something that might evade the eye
used to seeing what it always sees

I don't see
any of that but can feel
thunder
beneath my feet

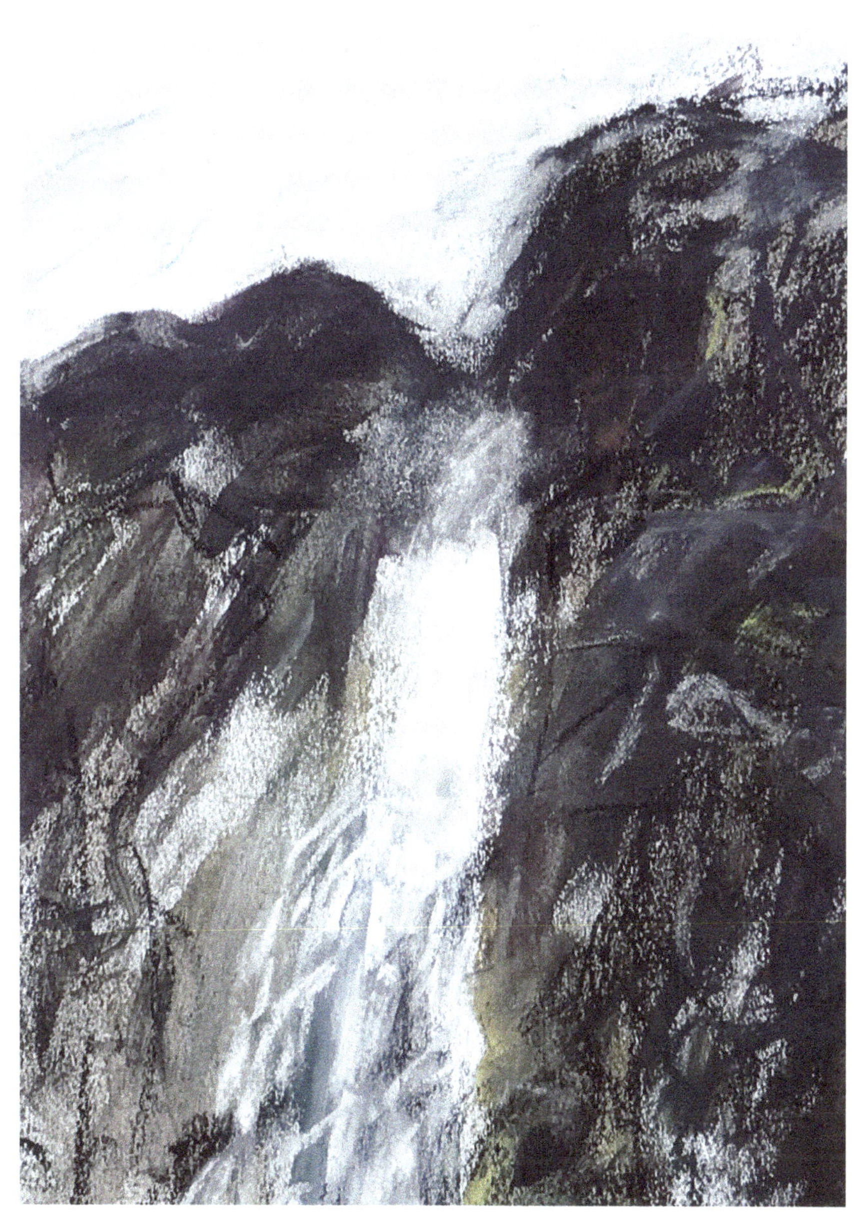

the intention

I'm in alpine territory
above the tree line
the last clump of beech

I can follow the intention
of the hills, all the way down
to distant green
or back up towards
the promise of snow

moss and rock sing
gravity glides
wind scars the slopes
the sky turns dark honey

there is no horizon
earth and sky just overlap
lips joined in open secrecy

I can lie down here, go soft
on the hard rock
and let the mountain do the dreaming

CRESCENT VALLEY

Look in the other way of looking
(Rumi)

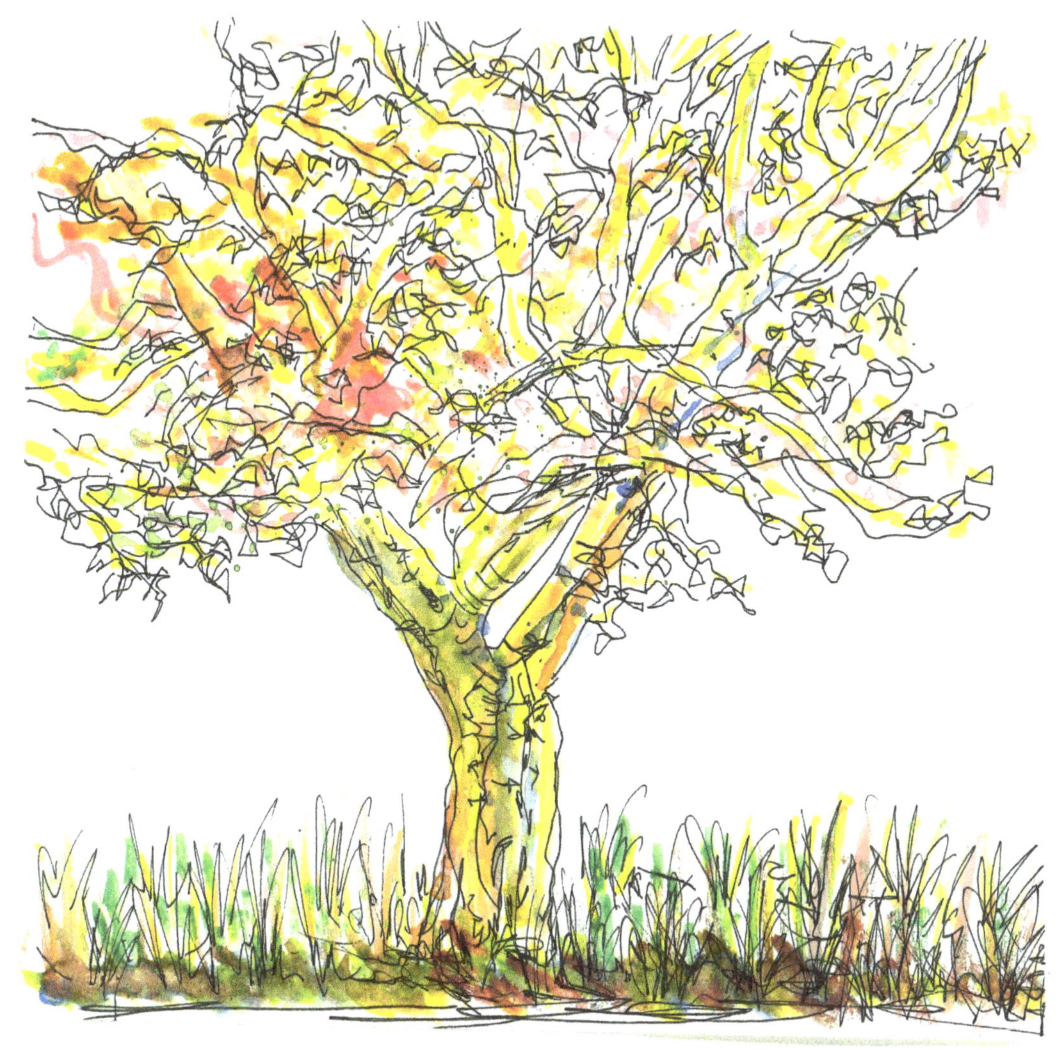

ripe fruit

our plum tree is in bloom
white fanned against the green

I used to sit beneath it
and wonder what it would be like
to sit beneath it
as I grew old
and it grew young again
every year

I don't have to wonder anymore
I grew old before the blossom
had faded from the branch
and died before the first leaf
turned green

now the tree is in bloom again
and I lift my limbs into the sky
waiting for the kereru to come
and fluster and bluster
amid my blossoms
anticipating ripe fruit

goblin party
(For Christina Rossetti)

when the night
puts the day away
the invisible ones come out to play

they sing and dance
and have their say
you can see them pass this way

when the night
puts the ranks of day to flight
and up there steals a softer light
you will see a most comical sight

right to left and left to right
off they march, off they prance
they sing and dance
and skip and pray
look and see them pass this way

going for a walk in the age of Covid 19

the first thing to notice
is the quiet

we can hear the tūī
call
from the other side
of the valley

we can hear the leaves
prattling to the wind
and the wind
brushing against the sky

the sprung rhythm of
the pōhutukawa branches
and a sprinkle of flower voices
light and airy
asking when there will be rain

how deep and sweet
silence can be
in the absence of the
acrid clatter
of petrol engines

the silence begins to repair itself
my footfalls
soft and steady

an empty road always looks longer
an empty sky always looks bluer

up ahead I see another human being
a vector!
I prepare for evasive action
the silence takes over both of us

as we pass
our footfalls mingle

this stealthy apocalypse
is giving nature around us
a bit of a breather
the wind has scraped away
the oily taste in the air

I get a text from a mate
'this is goodie, just like this place
used to be
before everything else'

the consolations of art

I can see across our valley
to the far side
where the gilded afternoon sun falls
as if it were a still life
best admired from a distance

see the kingfisher turn
into a star
as the world becomes
a stained-glass window
by Marc Chagall

like the starling sounds
of morning
like a couple holding hands
on an empty road
my words are happy enough
in their own bubble

once a great sage asked
what can a dog find in the darkness
of its own box?

after a thousand years of self isolation
I found the answer:
familiar smells

walking Crescent Road
at night

you can look up
to a narrow streak of stars
hemmed in by overarching
shadows
and trust your feet

close your eyes
and the world hardly changes
look to the left and right
nothing
but shades within shades
thoughts within thoughts
far from the tyranny of outlines
and the certainty of street

and you carry the moment eternal
with you, until you get to
the corner

our bush bathroom

a glass lotus flower
hangs in our bathroom window
turning from blue to green
and green to blue
as it moves in the wind

we have an old bathtub
that doesn't go anywhere
scattered with leaves and twigs
with iron claws for feet

in the corner, a pair of work boots
with exhausted looking socks
hanging in there
looking for a way out

there's a large window frame
with no glass
so the world can come
right on in
without being asked

there's a blackbird
keeping a nimble eye on things
who will hop in and
peck at the soap
given half a chance

and there's a person here too
standing in the shower, motionless
like a statue made of flesh
water born
singing of love

passing through

tūī arrives to drink from the spouting
blackbird flies in through the open window
and scratches around on the kitchen bench
pīwakawaka flicks sideways
from glance to glance

thrush gives throat to the world
kererū performs an elegant dive
from blue to green

the end of the day may fall into place
with a basketful of ripe plums
half-pecked
and some regrets

the armies of night
return home, their helmets blazing
a snarl of traffic at the roundabout

the soft-winged ruru flies by night
an old moon lies in the arms of the young

Te Toki

you find the scene you want
a mingimingi with tiny leaves
comingled by light
bark covered in runes and signs

after the rain the ground is funky
from wet leaves
and mossy afterthoughts
we could make love right here
just a few meters from the track
if the light were not so sneaky
and the mosquitoes more forgiving

instead you sketch stroke by stroke
while I sit
making squeaky seagull sounds
with a piece of grass between my thumbs
as my mother taught me
crying out for the forgotten ones
who cannot answer back

the tīpuna gather around
but I don't trust them
they carry too much of the world
for the dead to bear or the living to hold

I can't help them
or seek to join their ranks
or add my cries to theirs
seeking redress
for all those wrongs

it doesn't take long
for your sketch to be done
and for me to call up the kākā
from its hiding place in the sky
with my blade of stretched grass

the slender mapou dreams in light green
the afternoon sun calls it quits
and pulls its song from the shadows

writing in the rain

*

I'm trying to locate some helpful words
but my ears are too cold and my bones
have forgotten how to hold themselves
or how to remember where I came from
while the faces the future puts on
won't stay the course

*

the pied cormorant hasn't forgotten
how to fly, how to hold its wings
in natural balance
as it phases in and out of low hung mist
(we called them shags when I was young
and new to words)

*

we can't see the coastine from here
the coast is long gone
but we know it's there, beyond
the gasp of the heart
and saturated pages

*

the delicate paspalum
talks to itself
as it grows heavy

*

an empty bus rattles into the night
I can see my face in the passing dark
a pointillist portrait on glass
when was that? I wonder

to the valley below

you slip off down the valley
into the chill and dark
to write your words, do
your art

swift and silent
the ruru flies with you
prescient and wide-eyed

the territory before
the territory behind

garden devas wait
for that old elf moon to sink
and for the spirits that sing
to rise and play their part
hard sometimes to know where
to end or where to start
the feathery calm of the stars
the turbulent heart
perfumed fate
or passion-scribbled sheets

you wait
hiding in the rhyme
hiding in the line
in the opacity of the ink
and the murk of memory
with breath on the wing
holding that space
for the flare and
spark

a trick of the eye

outside my window
there's a tūī
sliding
with quick, deft movements
between the pink branches
of the spring plum
with a touch of white blossom at its throat

LET THERE BE

But because I ask for silence
don't think I'm going to die
The opposite is true;
it happens I'm going to live
(Pablo Neruda)

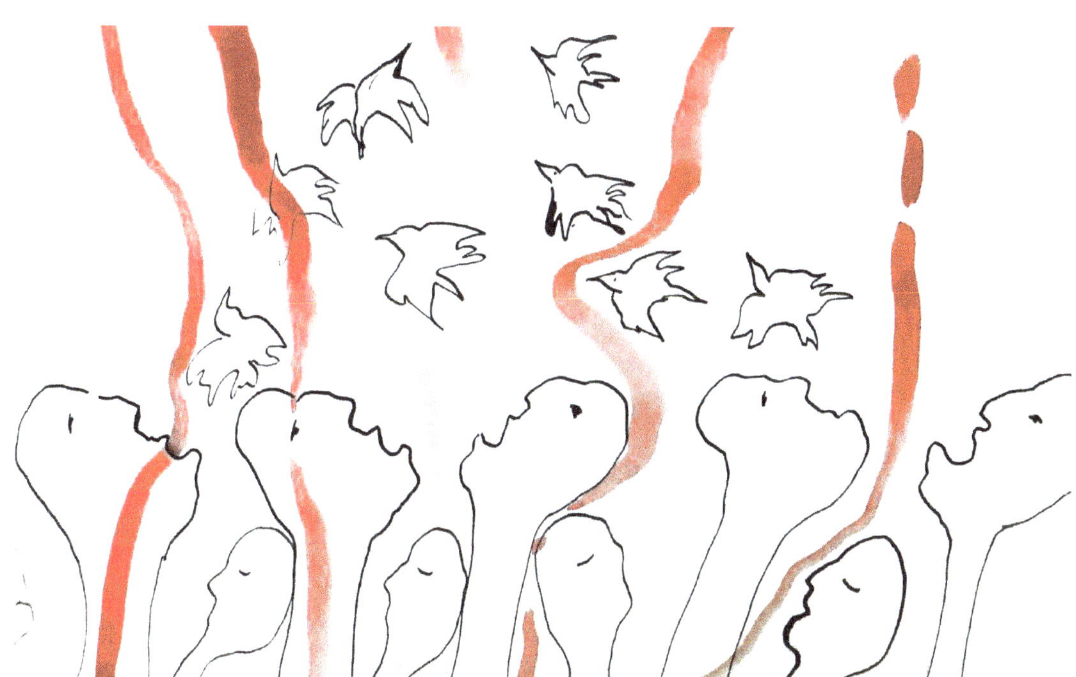

the ritual

morning breaks into
a chaos of blue
rocking-horse fragments
make believe when
there's no other kind

the procession winds its way
through the years, through
the streets
and through
the hearts of humankind

night is ravished
the shadows retreat to their lairs
a dawn chorus of singing leaves

from voice to voice
the chant goes to and fro
from flower to flower
and god to god
to haunt the years
the streets
and the hearts of humankind

rubbing sleeping birds from their eyes
people come to their doors
and their glass cages
to stand at their gates
to watch and listen
with wonder untold, and fear
in their bellies

as the dead approach
in their swirl and doom
who, with their saucer eyes
see right into the blue
and the years and the streets
and the hearts of humankind

let there be: to Pablo Neruda

now I can ask for a thousand silences
a thousand thousand silences
the silences of innumerable worlds
where all things live, make their play
and fade away

the inward silence of the nīkau grove
the outward silence of the empty street
the busy silence of vacant tongues
the crimson silence of the rose
the hopeful silence of a prayer
the cosmic silence of meditating stone
the potent, sprung silence of the seed
the complicated silence of the forest
the long silence of the pendulum
the sudden silence of the guillotine
the deep silence of a kiss
the rowdy silence of a South American novel
the seductive silence of a Neruda poem
the resonant silence of a quiet mind

the secrecy of water
the hush of frost
the stealth of dawn
the solitude of love

whatever silences you happen upon
let them all be

the big bang took place
in noiseless space

those who have come
this far
will hold each other
for all time, and longer
and lie together
flesh on star

reticent lovers
in their speechlessness

at long last I can ask for all those silences
that eluded me for so long
that got lost between the other bits
the this and the this
like the missing notes that fell
between the keys
when I should have been listening

now I can ask
for a thousand silences
and let the rest
rest

quite another poem

the dog across the way
enters the poem by means
of constant barking
where silence would have served
our purpose with ease

the sun comes into the lines
by means of the dawn
with a preference for definitions
when night's dreams
have not yet run their course

the voice of the radio intrudes
with tales of mayhem and madness
plague deaths and hate words
when a little ambient music
might have soothed the soul

the kawakawa across the way
slips into view by means
of a quiet strength and a healing voice
when a grand rata in full bloom
would have gone down a treat

the girl who often visits
arrives by virtue of her beauty
velvet in the shadows, velvet
in the memory
when peace of mind would have served
to hush the heart

the road enters the poem
because the girl and the dog
and the voices of doom
run together along it
beneath the kawakawa tree
when a little less bustle would have
allowed a better focus

the sky has to be there
because all things happen under the sun
and are irreversible, irresistible
irreplaceable
when a little soft darkness
would have been just the ticket

the earth has to be there
where the trees make a stand
and water limps from the hills
when something a lot more ethereal
and strange
might better thrill the mind

now the elements are assembled
in the manner of a riddle
in the manner of the inscrutable
with chance playing the riddler
while dog, tree, girl, radio and road
conjoin with the earth
awaiting their cue
when quite another poem
more pertinent
would have sufficed

the insomniac

I get up at 2 a.m and wander about
like some old man who lost the night
but found his feet

mosquitoes have damned my sleep
with their whining
their obsessive fly-bys of my face
and those stinging memories
I don't want
the memories and the ache

why should I care
if the wind races around
tears my hair
or the stars go out of shape
I am shredded by sleeplessness
and a prophetic singing in my ears

I have already given myself over
to the hard hour
and walk past houses sunk deep
within themselves, curtains drawn
against the coming
of the dawn
and all those images that flee
ahead of time
one step ahead
of the fretful mind

I turn off the torch
and follow a more wandering light

I am tattered, I am whole
I am riddled, I am complete
I am dispersed, I am gathered
I am perforated in the perforated dark
strangely happy, a creature of air

and above all
awake

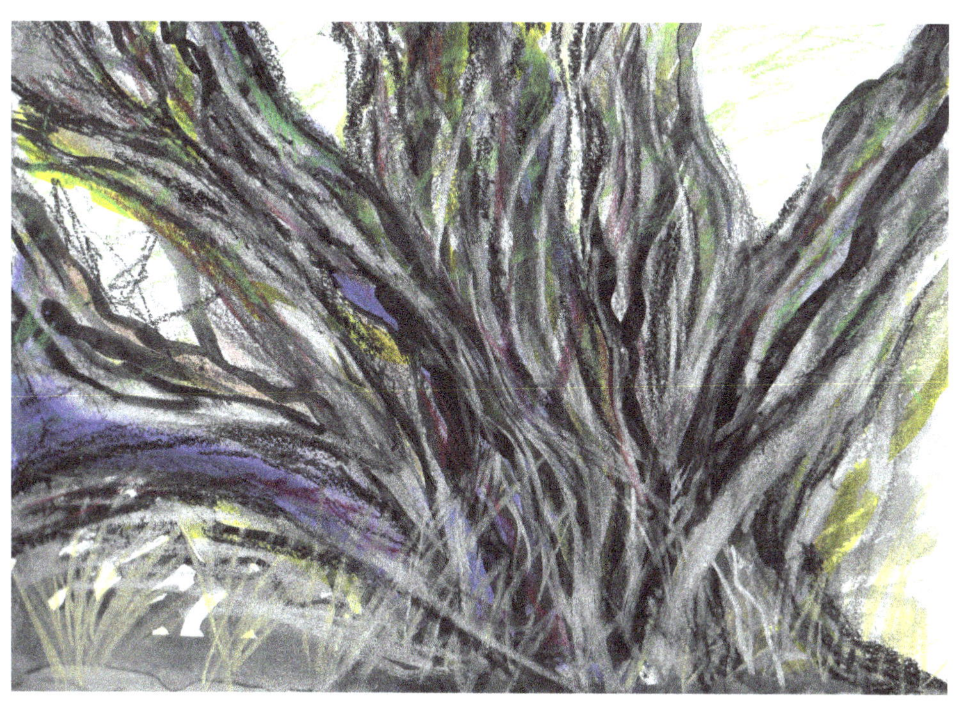

at Auckland Hospital

we are at the bottom
of a well of light

in a place with no shadows

*

we chat to keep away the silence
the dead walk on slippers

*

there are a lot of gaps to fill
or jump across

*

all the words are made of the same
structural grey steel

follow the yellow line

*

of this human suffering
no voice can tell
and perhaps there is some wonder here
after all
a miracle being wheeled somewhere
on a trolley bed

*

there's always somebody worse off
somebody says

*

coffee machine goes whoosh-sizzle

Lewy Body

"The past, like the future, is indefinite and
exists only as a spectrum of possibilities."
Stephen Hawking

he sits and mutters into his mouth
he's not really who he is, you know
or where he is, possibly in Ti Tree, or Hokitika
or washed up on a suitable bed
in Madrid, or on a train to Barcelona
where his wife is having an affair with the doctor
while an accordion plays gliding notes

he decides he might have lost his passport
on a ferry crossing years ago
or spent too long in Ashburton
before the lights went out
before that thought is replaced by another
something he seeks, some old sweet song
in the endlessness of the Canterbury Plains
under the flaming pillars of the nor-west arch
in the kingdom of icy peaks and ski freaks

the moment
never folds its wings

mist lies flat on the water
white porcelain sings

this ferry creates no wake, no waves
movement is notional
he is there, mixing his past with that of someone
who looks just like him
a fake without a face, and can't recall
what the time signature was

which dying fall, dark or fair
the notes he played on a button accordion
last forever in his hands, the Red River Valley
swells eternal through the staves

his bluntened hands do a Parkinson jig on the chair,
to those lines he never forgets
'*Then come sit by my side if you love me*
Do not hasten to bid me adieu...'
we might get stuck in the hall
but time doesn't, old insect time
runs ant circles around itself
we start but we can never catch up, and we can't
move our fingers fast enough over the keys

this hotel is on a lean, he says
they need to get the inspectors in
the floor suffers from undulation
a little coffee spills on his pants
so it looks like he's widdled himself
his hands dangle off the ends of his arms
like alien appendages
he sways in the blueberry wind

when he closes his eyes
trying to recall the tune
a candle flame crawls up the walls
like an ancient salamander
escaping the fires of creation
the juncture, this juncture
pulls both ways, forward and back
in and out, all at once, one foot forward
one foot slack

he has an owl moment
he is flickering through the night

he is looking for something lost
something shiny, in a minor key

there are holes where there should be an ocean
mist where there should be light
monsters come scurrying through
but they are all well medicated
so we don't take the ruins to heart
and there is some gleeful joke
at the end of Ariadne's thread
that returns us to the start
the first but final note

little lake

water lilies, pink and green
transform in the eye of a kingfisher
hiding in the shade

the brush hangs suspended above the page
the page drips white

in the still water, feeding mallards make a rippling
bubbling sound

te raupo, lean as spears
soft as grass

patterns of dust are stirred into shape
by the lightest of breezes
a mere breath

the air sibilates with the sound of cicadas
a pūkeko shouts a hoarse warning

the kānuka undulates on pillows of wind

the longer you look the more the world comes
into existence

if you gazed upon this little lake
as upon the face of a beloved
you would begin to see all the detail
and variations
all those things you failed to see at first
the hidden harmonies
the way the shadows slip between the light
and the way in which each and every element

falls into sweet accord
the dust-roughened water, the quick dragonfly
the raupō stepping out from the bank
all now
surrendered to the eye

at Found – Surfdale

154

the waitress writes our order
on the back of her hand
the fleshy part

gospel music
plays softly
while hot tea warms the soul

at the table, we have
a petunia moment
between words

I return to the beginning
but don't find myself there

a white dog wanders between the tables

LOVE AND CHAINS

But let's not talk of love
or chains
or things we can't untie
(Lenard Cohen)

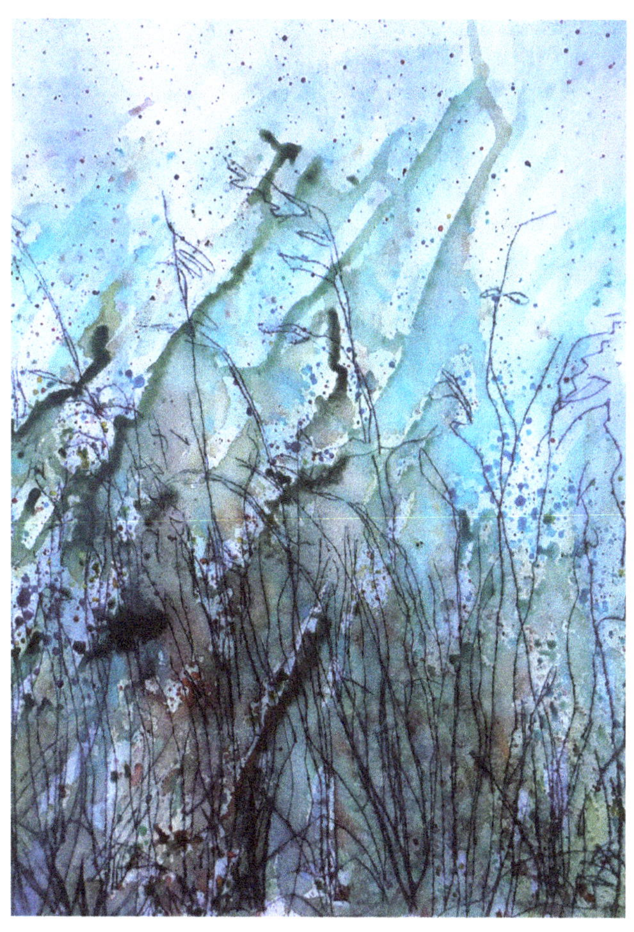

To L upon her coming out
as a bisexual

welcome, my love
to this long withheld truth
some things we can skirt around
for only so long

letting the old self die
the new skin hurts like hell
and people will say anything
you know
just for the hell of it

but know that you must fly with both your wings
or not at all
and if I cry its for all those years you fell
through the sky
trying to sing

plaything

it's all hither and yon
to and fro
obey or be obeyed
in this thistledown world

some wandering deity takes your life
and in one sharp breath
scatters it to the four winds

I see you in the garden
bent over the earth
planting marigolds

a feathered seed catches in your hair

girl with the red beret

as dark fell
you left your map on the table
where it had curled in the sun
with your eyeglass and sextant
a glass of lemonade going flat
and some aspects of a most intimate kind

a text message hanging in the air
like a hovering dragonfly

the girl with the red beret
puts silver glitter on her eyelids
but not too much
a creamy blouse with puffy sleeves
and white lace trimming
before hitting town
there'll be somebody around

here and there, a little flesh shows

she's your stranger
capering on invisible strings
signaling you to follow
into the burning world

you sketch her on her back
in black and white
arms stretched to each hemisphere
in slow rotation

you find yourself there
with memories of the coast
a dice throw of rocks
time's slow glass
a thin song
and another slab of colour
courtesy of daybreak

Return from P

you return
from the arms of your first world
that mirror place
where you meet yourself
and are taken by the unexpected
domesticity of a kiss

gods and children pass this way

don't know how I feel
about seeing you again in your cloak of mystery
cloak of invisibility
naked in memory,
wings from those skies
folded out of sight beneath ordinary shoulders
once more

shadows always return with dawn

while the door stands open
to all the winds of the world
and our bed lies empty
in the reflection of the window
and the kitchen smells of lost coffee
you disentangle yourself
from her soft touch
made fierce by time
and the tides of childhood
sands
and memories hard to bear
to return to the earth you know

and the man who stands
by the tree
holding up the house

Where are you tonight

sleep comes after me all purple and mauve
and turbid as rain
but I'm not there

the young oyster catcher
its back humped
runs begging after mother
for the rest of the world
the one that was promised
but mother isn't there
she's making a run for the horizon

bits of white and orange shell
beneath my feet
glow like a trail of stars
incandescent
but the chorus has gone home
to tea and storybooks

you search among the rocks
for a burnt stick
to catch the hard singing of the hills
but by the time you find it
our hearts have already broken
and mended
and broken again

later
I look for you in the dawn
coming up from the valley
up from your succulent visions
from the arms of your flower
your spiralling gardens

the jabberwocky scent of wet ponga
still on your hands

but the track must walk by itself
just this once
as there is nobody near
and I can barely hear
that far off song playing

slippery sparks

you come to my door
show me the stars
remote Andromeda, bright Sirius
and Mars

at the tips of our fingers
they are
well within reach yet impossibly far

we stand side-by-side
and plunge outwards
through the sidereal dark
a wild ride
to the light of distant suns
mere slippery sparks
in the evanescence of thought
as thought goes flying

all the while time gets older
its traces fade in worlds unmade
anchored here, on this lump of
orbiting rock

we stand together
yet apart
seeking our centre of gravity
above the galactic plane
our cosmological constant
in the silence and sadness
of the sharp glitter of eyes
abstracted and wise

and feel for the touch of
love
that leaves its mark

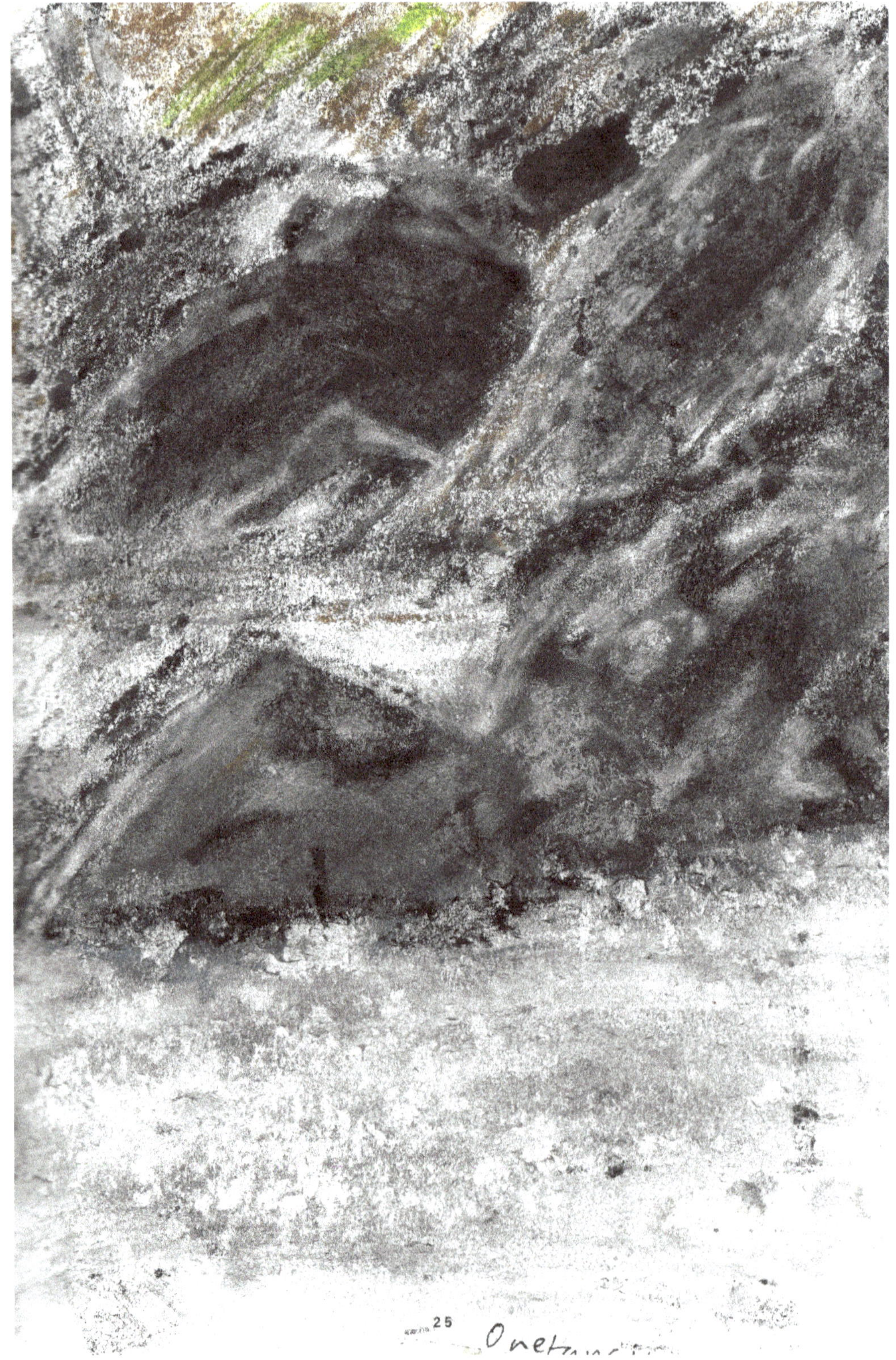

spring shadow

you've got to look in the other direction
to catch the creature
that most hidden creature
out of the corner of your eye
and only out of the corner of your eye
peeking through her lace
from her dark den
fingers curled
around her golden prey

she will come to you
in her own space
with her own fluid grace
in mythical lands where lips meet
and children play

along the roadsides, the wild onion
rings forth its white bells
and peach blossoms climb
into the sun
you've got to give a little
to get a little
they say
offer some to get some

linger by the corner of the sheet

I keep my love

I don't want the dawn
with its false promise
its lumpy hills
its grey, mediocre backwash
its trivial shadows
so easily pushed aside

I want a dark I can stroke
whisper to
feel my way into
the way a cat can slide
between impressions

I want a full, round, pregnant dark
whose byways are endless
whose houses drip with sleep
whose roads will always lead
to mysterious junctures
and whose coastlines are sketched
by the sea

I want a dark that is isotropic
that doesn't run out
that doesn't give way
that doesn't stumble
and in whose hug I may contain
everything that isn't, and will never be
defined

so I keep my love
of this fine-feathered darkness
even into the first cry of dawn
when it vanishes from our fingertips
and accursed light
pricks open the day

winter rain

when a gentle rain falls
we make amends

you were the first
and you will be the last
we tell each other
over tea and toast
as the dark lifts
and lovers line up for their kisses

it sounds good that way
a little green springs up
in our mind's eye
a little jump in the heart
at a touch
a soft bandage to the wound
the scent of creamy sandalwood
sweet horsetail
and sexy patchouli

the sky licks the earth
with a slushy tongue
the pond refills, and we wonder
if the slidey eel will return

tūī rejoice in the guttering
pīwakawaka come out to play
humans hold their heartbeat
in their hands

far off, a world sings
of love
and all that has been forgotten

we may not have the morrow
but we have the day
we tell ourselves
and the day has just begun

remnants

you can pour some wine on my grave
here among the pines
being dead is thirsty work

no one comes by much anymore
the lines on the page are few and far between
you'll have the place pretty much to yourself

all those memories have dried up
and blown away

A tall tree catches much wind

Note

I haven't much time
to dash this off
before you arrive

suddenly it's happening very fast
life and death flash by

landscapes flick in and out
like a lizard's tongue

I don't know if I'll get a space
to catch up with myself
let alone find you
in the mess of everything else

ps: sketchbook on the table
      plums in the fridge

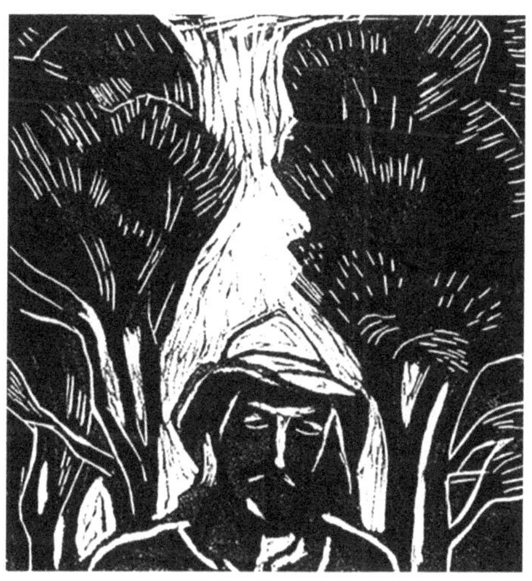

Mike Johnson, fiction writer and poet, is widely regarded as one of New Zealand's most innovative writers. He lives on Waiheke Island and has taught creative writing at AUT University and the University of Auckland. In 2002 he received The University of Auckland's Literary Fellowship, having been Literary Fellow at Canterbury University in 1987. His first novel, *Lear, the Shakespeare Company Plays Lear at Babylon* was short listed for the New Zealand Book Awards in 1986, his novel *Dumb Show* won the Buckland Memorial Award for Literary Excellence in 1995, and he won the Frances Kean Award his short story, 'Magic Strings' in 1999. His first book of poetry, *The Palanquin Ropes*, (1983) was co-winner of the John Cowie Reed Memorial Competition. His non-fiction, *Angel of Compassion*, was shortlisted for the Ashton Whyle Award in 2014, and a poem from *Vertical Harp, The selected poems of Li He* (2006) has been anthologised in the *Essential New Zealand Poems: Facing the Empty Page* (Random House, 2015). Mike Johnson is the author of twenty-six books including nine books of poetry, three of shorter fiction, one non fiction, three children's books, and ten novels.

Also by Mike Johnson

Novels
Stench
Driftdead
Lethal Dose
Zombie in a Spacesuit
Hold My Teeth While I Teach You to Dance
Travesty
Counterpart
Dumbshow
Antibody Positive
Lear: The Shakespeare Company Plays Lear at Babylon

Shorter Fiction
Confessions of a Cockroach/Headstone
Back in the Day: Tales of NZ's Own Paradise Island
Foreigners

Poetry
The Raising Light Trilogy
Ladder With No Rungs, Illustrated by Leila Lees
Two Lines and a Garden, Illustrated by Leila Lees
To Beatrice: Where We Crossed the Line
Vertical Harp: The Selected Poems of Li He
Treasure Hunt
Standing Wave
From a Woman in Mt Eden Prison & Drawing Lessons
The Palanquin Ropes

Non-Fiction
Angel of Compassion

Children's Books
Flippity Fluppity Flop, Illustrated by Daniela Gast
A House With No Windows, Illustrated by Ingrid Berzins
Kenni and the Roof Slide, Illustrated by Jennifer Rackham
Taniwha. Illustrated by Jennifer Rackham

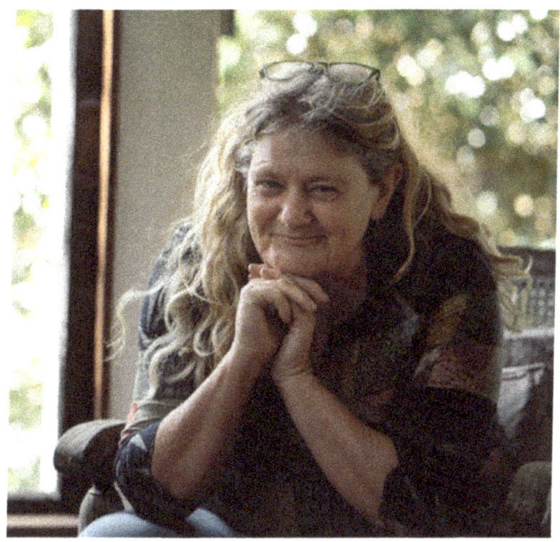

Leila Lees is an artist, poet and writer, living on Waiheke Island. She is an illustrator and printmaker, working in woodcut, monoprint, drypoint and mezzotint. Her art emerges from her sketchbook which is always at hand. Leila Lees's *Into the World* was the runner up in the Ashton Wylie Book Awards, 2019.

Also by Leila Lees

Books
Ferry Crossing
Piripai
The Little Book of Remedies
Into the World

Illustrations
Ladder With No Rungs
Two Lines And A Garden